Understanding Family Diversity and Home–School Relations

How can adults in early years settings and primary schools fully embrace the diverse nature of family life?

This essential text will help students and those already working with children to understand, both theoretically and practically, what may constitute a 'family'. It explores how to build relationships with a child's family to ensure early years settings and schools are working in partnership with children's home environments, thereby supporting the best possible learning outcomes for children.

It will help the reader to develop their skills, knowledge and understanding of their professional practice in education, and chapter by chapter explores the challenges that may be experienced in working with the diverse nature of family life in the UK, including:

- mixed race families;
- immigrant, refugee and asylum seeker families;
- step-families and step-parenting;
- gay and lesbian families;
- families and adoption;
- fostering and children in care;
- families living in poverty;
- families and bereavement; and
- families and disability (including mental health).

Understanding Family Diversity and Home–School Relations is engagingly practical, using case study examples throughout, and providing reflective activities to help the reader consider how to develop their practice in relation to the insights this book provides. It is a unique road-map to understanding pupils' backgrounds, attitudes and culture and will be essential reading for any student undertaking relevant Foundation and BA Degrees, including those in initial teacher training, taking post-graduate qualifications or as part of a practitioner's professional development.

Gianna Knowles is a senior lecturer in Educational Studies at the University of Chichester in the UK.

Radhika Holmström is a freelance journalist who specialises in covering diversity issues.

Understanding Family Diversity and Home–School Relations

A guide for students and practitioners in early years and primary settings

Gianna Knowles and Radhika Holmström

LONDON AND NEW YORK

First published 2013
by Routledge
2 Park Square, Milton Park, Abingdon, Oxon OX14 4RN

Simultaneously published in the USA and Canada
by Routledge
711 Third Avenue, New York, NY 10017

Routledge is an imprint of the Taylor & Francis Group, an informa business

© 2013 Gianna Knowles and Radhika Holmström

British Library Cataloguing in Publication Data
A catalogue record for this book is available from the British Library

Library of Congress Cataloging in Publication Data
Knowles, Gianna.
Understanding family diversity and home-school relations : a guide for
students and practitioners in early years and primary settings / Gianna
Knowles and Radhika Holmstrom.
pages cm
1. Home and school–Great Britain. 2. Families–Great Britain. I.
Holmstrom, Radhika. II. Title.
LC225.33G7K66 2012
371.19'20941–dc23
2012007577

ISBN: 978-0-415-69403-2 (hbk)
ISBN: 978-0-415-69404-9 (pbk)
ISBN: 978-0-203-15126-6 (ebk)

Typeset in Galliard by Prepress Projects Ltd, Perth, UK

MIX
Paper from
responsible sources
FSC
www.fsc.org   FSC® C004839

Printed and bound in Great Britain by
TJ International Ltd, Padstow, Cornwall

To Miriam and Naomi Sattar Holmström, who make family life diverting as well as diverse

Contents

Introduction

Radhika Holmström and Gianna Knowles

> We have found overwhelming evidence that children's life chances are most heavily predicated on their development in the first five years of life. It is family background, parental education, good parenting and the opportunities for learning and development in those crucial years that together matter more to children than money.
>
> (Field 2010, p. 5)

In 2010 the British government published *The Foundation Years: Preventing Poor Children Becoming Poor Adults. The Report of the Independent Review on Poverty and Life Chances* (Field 2010). The quote above details one of the main findings from the Field (2010) report. The report goes on to explore how the family unit in which children grow up is one of the central factors in determining a child's future life experience. The report also discusses the importance of good educational provision, from the earliest years, in enhancing a child's future well-being and life-chances. From this report we can see that, if children are to grow up to thrive as adults, those working with children in educational settings need to be in partnership with a child's family from the beginning, thereby ensuring children are able to make the most of the earliest educational opportunities they are presented with.

Before a child enters any educational setting they have already learnt many things from their family. From the very first moments of life children begin to learn how to live in the society they are growing up into. As they develop, children learn the attitudes, values and beliefs their family holds and these will come to the early years (EY) setting and primary school with them. They will impact on the day-to-day experiences of a child's early life and often these influences will form part of a child's identity and be a hugely determining feature throughout a child's whole life. These influences will impact on how 'ready to learn' a child is when they start school and, as Field states: 'a child's home environment affects their chances of being ready to take full advantage of their schooling' (Field 2010, p. 5).

Most families are very keen to be involved in their children's education; however, sometimes there can be a mismatch between the EY setting's or school's view of what should be happening under the umbrella term of education. Where these tensions arise families can feel their values and beliefs about education are being ignored or marginalised and the EY settings and schools can feel the families are being difficult, or do not care about the education of their children. There are many reasons why tensions over education between EY settings, schools and families can occur, one of them being that EY settings and schools may not fully appreciate the nature of the family background supporting the child and therefore not understand how best to engage with that family.

Some of the tension between educational settings and families occurs because, for many years, there has been a common widespread assumption that when the term 'family' is used, what that term means is 'a particular type of relationship and parenting . . . a heterosexual union within marriage' (Chambers 2001, p. 6); a family unit in which the children in the family are from that heterosexual marriage and, ideally, the father in the family goes out to work while the mother's role is to be the homemaker. Indeed, many families are constituted in this way; however, as Chambers discusses, for some children this type of family arrangement 'has only ever existed as a transitional phase of some people's lives' (Chambers 2001, p. 1). What is more often the case is that the term 'family' actually refers to 'a variety of living arrangements . . . being experienced in western nations, including some complex multiple-occupancy households that have not, as yet, been given a satisfactory label' (ibid.).

It is the relationship between EY settings, schools and these 'complex multiple-occupancy households', or families, which this book seeks to explore. Early years settings and schools are very practised at working alongside conventional families to promote children's learning, yet sometimes forget to consider the ways in which other family groups need to be engaged to ensure the education of children from these families is also being promoted. Notions of family that depart from the dominant discourse of the 'traditional' nuclear family module, a concept discussed in Chapter 1 of this book, can often be overlooked or depicted in quite negative terms. In practice, as many working in EY settings and schools are aware, it is more complicated than this. Children come from a huge range of families, and their family make-up interacts with children's experience of education in complex ways.

To ensure that children get the best educational start in life, as we will discuss later in the book, we must also consider research which has shown that some families are better placed than others to provide children with the social and cultural capital they need to take full advantage of the educational opportunities available to them. For children without these family advantages it may be up to the EY settings and schools to make up that difference for these children, particularly if they are able to offer social mobility, through education, to all children.

It is also important to remember that children are not passive in the experience of being a child and growing up. As Brannen discusses, children are 'reflexive, moral agents themselves' (Brannen *et al.* 2000, p. 10). That is to say, children have views and opinions and develop autonomously in response to what is happening around them. They 'make sense of their experiences of parents' care and how they, as active co-contributors to care, interpret moral imperatives to care for, and to cooperate with, others' (ibid.). Children learn about life and how to behave and treat others, they learn what is of value, what attitudes and beliefs to hold in response to the behaviours, values, attitudes and beliefs of those around them – both those who are family members and those they meet in educational settings. And although 'children may also have views' both about 'the nature of parenthood and parenting', they will also hold views about 'what it means to be a' 'child' and about the education they are receiving (Brannen 2000, p. 10). That is to say, as we work with children and their families, we need to remember that all in this relationship have a view about what should be happening and, for the partnership to work, all views need to be considered.

Sometimes books on families are not books about families. They are books structuring the discourse on family through promoting a particular model of what a family is. One of the results of having a rigid model of how a family should be is that those families that do not reflect this model, either because they cannot or will not, are treated as if they are aberrant or failing families. What this book aims to do is not to present a fixed notion of what a family should be, but to explore how families really are and to celebrate the strengths that are within those families. Most families will, at some time, experience stresses that will impact on all family members, including the children in those families. Sometimes there has been a temptation to believe that if only the family fitted the nuclear family model these stresses would go away, rather than recognising that it is not how the family is constituted that is the issue, but those factors causing the stress. This book explores how families actually are and the challenging circumstances that many families live with; it does this to seek to enable those working in schools to better understand how to build relationships with families that support children's learning and achievement in school.

For all the reasons listed above, this book aims to help students and those already working in the children's workforce to understand, both theoretically and practically, what may constitute a 'family' and how to build relationships with each child's family. Central to many of the discussions in this book are the themes of identity and belonging, attachment and loss. For many human beings, achieving well-being as an adult is linked to having a sense of identity, an understanding of who they are and how they belong to and fit within the community and society they live in. Similarly, to flourish, human beings need to be attached to and belong to other groups of human beings and to be able to form secure attachments with those around them. Many adults who did not have the opportunities to develop a sense of identity or form strong attachments, or who suffered loss as children and were unsupported in overcoming that loss, struggle to achieve well-being as adults. Families are where children learn about who they are, where they come from and the history and cultures they belong to. For a huge majority of children, leaving aside the normal ups and downs of family life, their families are also places where they learn to form strong and positive attachments and, where necessary, to grieve for losses they have suffered. Early years settings and schools need to be aware of how important identity and attachment are for children. If they are to enable children to make the most of the educational opportunities available, they need to be aware of how they are responding to the needs of children for whom the search for their identity may have been fragmented, perhaps because they are in care, and how, again, some family circumstances can lead to issues with attachment and loss.

In exploring all the themes briefly discussed above, Chapter 1 of the book sets the wider context these ideas are framed in. It starts the book by exploring the whole notion of what is meant by the term 'family' and why the concept of family is of enduring importance for children and society. It introduces the notion of attachment and discusses how children need to form secure attachments to enable them to thrive as adults. The chapter also introduces the notion of social capital and begins to explore why social capital is such a significant factor in educational achievement.

Having discussed the role of the family in enabling individual children to flourish, Chapter 2 discusses the wider social dimension of families. That is how families give children a sense of identity and teach them about their cultural heritage. The chapter explores what is sometimes seen as the tension between developing individual identity and having a responsibility to consider the needs of wider society, perhaps over and above personal wants and desires. The chapter also explores tensions in wider society with regard to cultural diversity, gender, identity and achievement in learning.

Chapter 3 is the first chapter that begins to look at these wider themes in terms of how they might relate to some specific family units, beginning with 'mixed race' families. The chapter explores what is meant by the term 'mixed race' and how 'mixed race' as a category is a growing ethnic group in the UK today. It examines the stereotypes and assumptions about mixed race children, their families, individual children's educational attainments and the challenge, for some children, of being mixed race and establishing an identity.

Some children in the UK experience life as an immigrant, asylum seeker or refugee. Chapter 4 discusses the experience of these children and explores how being a refugee or asylum seeker is different from being an immigrant. It looks at a recent history of migration to Britain and across Europe, as well as the more recent arrival of immigrants in the UK from Eastern Europe. It discusses who migrates to the UK and why and then begins to look at why families seek refuge or asylum and the specific challenges children from these families bring to their education.

Chapter 5 discusses step-families and step-parenting and how one in three people are in a step-family situation (Hayman 2001). It explores what is meant by step-parenting and step-families and the range and complexity of having 'step' relations. It discusses how children deal with disrupted attachments and form new attachments as families break up and reform, and how many children suffer feelings of loss as they go through this process. The chapter examines how dominant discourses about 'nuclear families' can marginalise the experience of those living in step-families.

In Chapter 6 what it means to be a gay or lesbian family and gay and lesbian parenting are explored. In particular, the chapter looks at the background and the facts about gay and lesbian families, as compared with some of the media myths that surround such families. It discusses how gay and lesbian families may be formed through surrogacy, artificial insemination and adoption and how individuals might work out roles and relationships in gay and lesbian families. Many children and adults in such families find that they have to deal with other people's sometimes negative assumptions, discrimination, a complex legislative framework and other people's reactions to their civil partnerships. The chapter explores how some families in this situation choose to be open about how their family is constituted, whereas others keep their relationships private.

The issue of families, disability and mental health are discussed in Chapter 7. In particular, the chapter explores what is meant by the term 'disability', including mental health challenges, and explores how families experience disability. It looks at how adults and children experience having a disability, the medical model of disability and the social model of disability. The chapter considers how having a disabled sibling, being a child carer or being a disabled parent can impact on the educational achievement of children. It discusses how disability in the family can lead to discrimination, poverty, hate crime and prejudice for some families.

For some children family life breaks down and they may be placed with foster families or live in other care situations. Chapter 8 details the number of children being fostered, or who are in other forms of care, and the impact of being a child in care on learning and achievement. It explores fostering and how to support fostered children and foster families. It explains why some children need to be in care and explores the challenges that children in care face in the education system.

Chapter 9 follows on from the previous chapter and explores families and adoption, discussing in particular what we mean by the term 'adoption' and what it means for a child to be adopted. It looks at reasons why children in the UK enter the adoption system, who can adopt and children's right to contact with birth parents. The chapter explores inter-country adoption and how children deal with the loss of birth families and form attachments to new families. In its final section the chapter looks at working with adoptive parents and adopted children's experience in the education system.

Chapter 10 discusses the issue of families living in poverty, exploring what it means for a child to live in poverty and how poverty impacts on social mobility, social capital and long-term *life chances*. It discusses those more at risk of living in poverty and how we can prevent poor children from becoming poor adults.

The final chapter in the book, Chapter 11, explores families and bereavement, looking at the incidence of children who are bereaved, having lost a close family member. It discusses the different ways grief may be expressed and why being bereaved as a child can have such an impact on learning. The chapter examines cultural and gender differences in dealing with bereavement and how to help a child cope when they lose a parent or sibling. Supporting children bereaved by a death due to suicide, or experiencing loss because of family breakdown, is also explored.

1 Families, home–school relations and achievement

Gianna Knowles

This chapter explores:

- what is meant by the term 'family' and why the concept of family is of enduring importance for children and society;
- the concept that children need to form secure attachments when young to enable them to thrive, and the role of the family in this process;
- how families provide children with the social capital to enable them to thrive in school and as adults;
- the role of the school in providing equality of opportunity for children to achieve.

What do we mean by 'family' and why are families important for children and the whole of society?

This chapter begins by exploring the notion of what we mean when we talk of 'family'. Much of the work early years (EY) settings and primary schools are engaged in is closely linked with children and their families. Therefore, in seeking to enable the best learning environments and support for children to achieve at school we know we need to be working closely with children's families too. As we will explore, what is meant by 'family' can vary from person to person and any one view of what a family is can often be linked to personal experiences of family. However, as with many aspects of our professional lives we know that to ensure we are providing the best support for children we need to be able to think in the broadest terms about children's lives, interests and experiences. Therefore, for our own professional development we need to think through the range of family experiences and backgrounds the children we work with may come from and learn how children's family circumstances will impact on their approach to and engagement with their learning at school.

Families are important, both for individuals and for society as a whole. As Bernardes (1997, p. 1) writes: 'for most of our lives, "our family" is the most important thing of all'. Even where family life breaks down and children are taken into care, or where families become dispersed (because of the need to flee to another country and seek refuge or asylum, for example) or separated because of illness and bereavement, still, most people grow up having had some connection to a group of people that they will think of as family. Most of us are 'born into families and spend, whether we choose or not, most of our childhood and teenage years within "our family"' (ibid.).

In this way, families are a fundamental part of the educational process for children. As well as being there to support children in being successful at school, families can also have a lasting impact on shaping the formation of an individual's identity, including giving many of the attitudes, values and beliefs an individual will hold as an adult. Sometimes an individual will continue to uphold and live by the values, attitudes and beliefs that they learnt from their families, and sometimes they may choose to modify some or all of the ideas they learnt from their family. As well as helping an individual to form the values, attitudes and beliefs to live their lives by, families are also good training grounds for learning about how to form relationships, deal with conflict and live with others.

For the reasons just discussed, in a very pragmatic way and from a wider societal point of view, society could not survive without families. Most families seek to provide love and care for those within their family group, however it is constituted, and most families generally want the best outcomes for the children in the family with regard to education (Brannen *et al.* 2000). Families also teach children the way the society they are growing up in 'works' and, in this way, teach children to become the future adults of that society (Abbott and Langston 2006). However, this is not to say all families have the same values, attitudes and beliefs about how to 'bring up children', what school is about or how to be an adult. The general point that is being made here is that society needs families, as there is no better way for a society to find the day-to-day, minute-by-minute work that families do to support their family members and raise the children within those families, on the scale needed across the whole of society.

As we have said, most families provide the emotional and physical care individual family members need to thrive, because of their love for and commitment to the members of their family. However, although all members of society profit from the work done by families, wider society can sometimes fail to acknowledge the range of ways families can be constituted. If society's views, as often expressed through the media, focus on only a limited notion of what is meant by the term 'family', the family experience of many children can be overlooked and marginalised. In turn, limited ideas about what the term 'family' can mean can encourage those working with children in EY settings and schools to fail to understand and connect with some of the families they need to work alongside, as they fail to recognise particular home set-ups or units as legitimate families. From a child's point of view, the family unit they live in is what families are. Children have no preconceived ideas about how families 'should be' and failing to connect with a child's family, because it does not fit a view of what a family should be, can be damaging both to a child's self-esteem and to their capacity to engage with education.

That society is concerned about the role and importance of families is an idea often discussed in the media. However, there is a current dominant discourse, or collective idea, that somehow family life in the UK is in a state of chaos and that this is contributing to wider societal breakdown. As the *Daily Mail* newspaper states: 'Yes family breakdown IS behind broken Britain' (Ware 2009).

Reflective activity

Consider the following newspaper headline, 'Duncan Smith blames riots on family breakdown':

> The work and pensions secretary, Iain Duncan Smith, has blamed the summer riots in England on family breakdown and a benefit system that has helped generate a 'growing underclass' of people living unproductive lives . . . Saying gangs had played a significant part in the riots, he said tackling the UK's violent gang culture was vital and that restoring the economy should go 'hand in hand with restoring society'.
>
> (Mulholland 2011)

Compare the headline and article above with the following statement:

> gangs have been a feature of the British landscape for centuries . . . in the 19th century, groups of boys lived independently of their parents, sometimes in settings not unlike those portrayed by Dickens in his Oliver Twist.
>
> (Covey 2010, p. 78)

Consider this newspaper headline:

> It's not just absent fathers, Mr Cameron. Family breakdown is driven by single mothers on benefits.
>
> (Phillips 2011)

Compare it with the following comment:

> the 19th century was a period of energetic marital non-conformity amongst couples of all social classes . . . In general, between 1760 and 1840 cohabitation seemed more widespread than in the mid 19th century and after 1880 attitudes towards sexual non-conformity became freer once again. Widespread practice of cohabitation

has only taken place since the 1970s in Britain but many couples, albeit only a minority, chose to participate in free unions for many hundreds of years before then.

(Frost 2008, p. 1)

Think about your family and the families of your friends. What families that you know of would you describe as having broken down to such an extent that they are causing wider societal breakdown? Your family and the other families you know may not fit a storybook notion of 'family'; however, the reality is that there has never been one way of constituting a family and there have always been those who live on the margins of society who cause harm and violence to others; you may know some individuals like this, but they are likely to be the exceptions rather than the rule. The important thing here is to disentangle the myths about family life and societal breakdown from the reality and to consider the rich, successful diversity of family life in Britain and to understand how to work with that diversity to promote educational achievement.

Exploring the range of ways families can be constituted, how and why families are so different, both in their make-up and sometimes in the way they approach life and looking after their children, is a significant part of what this book is aiming to explore. It is intended that, through having a greater understanding of these issues, those working with children, or intending to work with children in an educational setting, will be better able to connect with and support the learning of the children in their care.

To begin to unpick why there is such diversity in what constitutes people's notion of family and why there is such a diversity of family groupings in Britain, it is perhaps helpful to look briefly at some of the recent social history of the UK. As for many countries the twentieth century saw a time of huge social change for Britain (Schwab *et al.* 2000; Abbott and Langston 2006); to a greater extent this was as a result of Britain's involvement in the two world wars of 1914–18 and 1939–45. The devastation and privation of the actual wartime periods, and of the subsequent post-war eras, saw notions of the structures and functions of particular hierarchies, and of groups in society, change. After 1918 old notions of the authority of moneyed and hereditary privilege began to rapidly disappear. It was recognised that all should be valued on their own merit, not because of the class they were born into or the money they had. The notion that women and girls had a role in wider society equal to and as valuable as that of men also began to gain greater ground. After 1945 Britain began to develop its welfare system, providing good education and free health care for all. The necessity of rebuilding Britain's immediate post-war shattered industries and infrastructures saw the beginning of the movement of people and families from Britain's former colonies to the UK. More recent economic events in Europe and Britain's involvement in wars in the Middle East have also increased the number of people and families moving to the UK for work and asylum.

Alongside these social changes the twentieth century saw considerable technological change, in industry, the home and the media. And although poverty is still an issue for many in the UK and for British society as a whole, generally, since 1945 many have benefitted from an improved standard of living (Foley *et al.* 2001; World Bank 2010). The issue of families living in poverty is more closely explored in Chapter 10. Increase in income, access to education for all sectors of society and the greater possibility for more to pursue education to a higher level; increase in the diversity of cultural ideas and traditions and the huge range of lifestyle choices available and constantly being celebrated and presented by the media – these have also prompted people to consider, and to be able to finance, a range of ways that lives can be lived and families constituted. Where such choice is available, affordable and possible, so is the scope for what might be termed 'family' and the possibility for families to move away from a more rigid conception of what 'family' might be, than was perhaps the case up to the 1980s (Chambers 2001).

Change in societies is not new, or special to the twentieth century; however, it is sometimes helpful to pause and reflect on recent events, since change brings with it the need to consider and sometimes re-evaluate a whole range of ideas and perspectives, to see if they 'fit' with the new or current landscape. In this way, one of the purposes of this book is to allow the reader to reflect on and to evaluate or re-evaluate where we are in terms of our understanding of what we mean by the term 'family'. That it is important to do this, particularly for those working with children, is because research, including government research, shows that a child's family 'affects their chances of being ready to take full advantage of their schooling' (Field 2010, p. 5). A child's 'home environment' (ibid.) is the single most important factor that influences how children will engage with and achieve in their learning.

For many years there has been a notion that when families were talked about, in the media, in schools and by government, the family model they had in mind was what is often called the 'nuclear family' (Chambers 2001). Generally what is meant by the nuclear family can be described as:

> a young, similarly aged, White, married heterosexual couple with a small number of healthy children living in an adequate home. There is a clear division of responsibilities in which the male is primarily the full-time breadwinner and the female primarily the caregiver and perhaps a part-time or occasional income earner.
>
> (Bernardes 1997, p. 3)

Although many families in the UK will reflect this notion or model of what is meant by family, there are just as many families that are constituted in a completely different way.

Reflective activity

Chambers (2001) discusses how society has come to change its notion of what it means by 'family' as increasingly 'evidence of the widespread nature of divorce, remarriage, post-divorce families, single parenthood, joint custody, abortion, cohabitation and two career families' (Chambers 2001, p. 17) has become a more usual model of family groups, rather than the exception.

Consider your own family. Of those you would describe as members of your family, or part of your family, who do you consider as being family because you are related to them biologically? Who do you consider as family because of other strong relationships you have built with them?

Consider your friends and their families. How many of them live in families that fit the notion of the nuclear family model?

From the point of view of any individual thinking about their family: 'families are families, whether birth, extended, adoptive, foster, or step-families, and they can be very damaging or healing in their attitudes and interactions' (Raicar 2009, p. 198). The subsequent chapters in this book will further explore some of the ways in which families can be constituted and the strengths and challenges of these family groupings, and how those working in education can ensure they are connecting with children's families. Below is an exercise to help you begin to think about how EY settings and schools approach their role in connecting with children's families, to ensure educational achievement is supported as well as it can be.

Reflective activity

Early years settings and primary schools work hard to encourage the families they work with to be partners in supporting children's learning. However, it is always helpful to review and update provision from time to time to ensure it is meeting the objectives intended. Give some thought to good practice in working with families you have seen in an EY setting or primary school.

Give three examples of what you consider to be 'good' about this practice.

In 2010 the Department for Education canvassed the opinions of families across the UK to find out what was working well for them in terms of being involved in their child's education. Consider some of the following findings from the report (DFE 2010, p. 31):

A third of parents (34 per cent) said they were 'always confident' helping their child with homework. However, this confidence declines as children get older.

Mothers working full time (14 per cent) were more likely than fathers working full time (seven per cent) to help children with their homework every day.

41 per cent of fathers . . . and 41 per cent of mothers . . . agreed that it is more difficult for fathers to get involved in their children's learning.

'A third of parents (32 per cent) wanted to be more involved in their child's school life'. In particular, those who felt they did not have as much involvement as they would like were parents, particularly fathers, who were not living in the same house as their children (DFE 2010, p. 31).

Review the practice you were thinking about at the beginning of this exercise. What examples can you think of where the fathers and men in children's lives are actively encouraged to be part of the child's education? How does your practice help the two-thirds of families that are not confident in helping children with their homework?

Attachment theory

With respect to children thriving and achieving at school, as we have already begun to explore, research consistently shows that it is not necessarily how a family is constituted that makes the difference, but the nature of the secure attachments and support the child receives from its home and family. In its publication *A New Approach to Child Poverty: Tackling the Causes of Disadvantage and Transforming Families' Lives* (HM Government 2011) the government emphasises the importance of children having 'supporting strong, stable families' (ibid., p. 35), particularly if they are also to have 'positive home learning . . . environments' too (ibid.). It has long been recognised that one of the most important things children need to thrive and flourish are capable, loving and caring persons around them with whom they can form mutual supportive attachments (Mayseless 2002; Prior 2006). Whether these capable, loving and caring persons are related to the child by birth is not as important as the capacity of the people around the child, including siblings, to provide the nurture and support needed to enable the child to thrive.

Much of our current understanding of attachment theory derives from the work of John Bowlby, who was writing and researching in this field in the 1960s and 1970s (Prior 2006). Bowlby's notion of attachment explores how infant humans need to form relationships with those around them who are providing for their immediate needs of hunger, warmth and comfort. For most babies, these relationships develop into mutually affectionate and rewarding bonds for both the infant and the caregivers. It is when these bonds are not formed appropriately that children may grow up exhibiting signs of attachment disorders and behavioural challenges (Mayseless 2002; Prior 2006). From the age of two or three, infants begin to understand that the others around them are separate persons who also have their own needs and wants and they begin to develop relationships with a wider range of others, both children and adults, friends, teachers and so on. As children grow through childhood and adolescence into young adulthood the initial attachments begin to be overtaken by other relationships, including, as they become young adults, more intimate partnerships. Indeed, it could be argued that it is part of the role of the family to provide the initial attachments and to allow the child to 'grow away' to form strong, secure adult relationships, which often, in turn, become stable partnerships and new families. Raicar (2009, p. 33) explains how: 'anger, crying, cooing, calling, clinging, smiling at, or following/keeping close to an attachment figure are all spontaneous biologically inherited attachment behaviours'. What is more: 'these attachment behaviours can be attractive to carers and, thus, encouraged and so reinforced, establishing learnt patterns of interaction for the child' (ibid.). In this way even very young babies will learn what they need to do to get the attention from those around them.

When Bowlby first began developing attachment theory much of his writing discussed the importance of the initial attachment bonds being between the infant and its mother – ideally the baby's birth mother. Some have argued that this stance has served to further support the notion of the nuclear family model, as outlined by Bernardes (1997) above, as being the best way a family should be constituted. However, as Bowlby's theory of attachment began to be further developed and explored it was shown that it does not matter who the child initially attaches to; indeed there can be a number of attachment figures. What is of most importance is that the attachment figure or figures not only provide for the infant's primary needs, but ideally also provide love, care and affection (Prior 2006; Knowles and Lander 2011). Attachment theory also discusses how, as babies grow into children and children into teenagers and then young adults, the nature of these attachment relationships change and those individuals adapt to changes. In this way, children move from close relationships with parent figures to friendships with other children and then, as young adults, intimate relationships with other adults.

In terms of educational achievement, children who have formed secure attachments and have families around them who are caring, loving and nurturing are more likely to engage with their learning. They are more likely to come to the setting or school with a positive attitude and be 'ready to learn'.

In families in which there are strong attachments of the kinds described, it is also likely that those providing the care for the child want to be involved in helping the child achieve. In this way, EY settings and schools need to be sensitive to who it is they need to work with in the family to support a child's learning.

Reflective activity

Think back over your life. Who were the most important people to you when you were a child? Who do you feel you have the closest relationships with now? How have your relationships changed over time? Of the people you feel closest to, how many of them are you related to by birth?

You and the adults around you will have grown up in families constituted in many different ways. For example, they may be families in which one adult, who may or may not have been a birth parent, may have been responsible for the family unit. Similarly, you or the adults and children around you may have family units supported by older siblings or step-parents. Family groups may contain step-brothers and sisters, or half-brothers and sisters. Aunts, uncles and grandparents may be integral family members having parental responsibility, morally and financially, if not legally, for other family members. There will be families comprising same-sex couples or families that have experience of being part of foster families, in care or with an adopted family.

In the same way that there are families that do not 'fit' the nuclear family model in terms of the way they are composed, there are also families that sometimes go unrecognised, or are marginalised because they are 'different' in that they are mixed race families, have an ill or disabled family member, are families new to Britain (which have come to the UK seeking refuge or asylum) or are families experiencing a bereavement. Therefore, although the term 'family' can mean many different things, what is of central importance about a group of people who define themselves as a family is that the family members' primary needs of food, shelter and safety are being provided for. In addition to this, for the members of that family to fully thrive, there is love, care and affection too, enabling attachments to be formed that will nurture and support those within the family.

Reflective activity

Tom is seven. He lives with his mum and his sister, who is 14. Lately he has been turning up at school late and has not been engaging with his school work. He has seemed distant, even in the playground, where he has not been playing with his friends. Often, Tom seems tired and he has been very hungry by lunchtime, and is beginning to look uncared for.

What might be all the possible causes of the change in Tom?

One day one of the children said Tom was crying in the playground; a teaching assistant working in Tom's class found a quiet place to have a chat with him. Tom said that his granddad had been ill and had been going to the hospital and now his hair had fallen out and he stayed in bed a lot. Tom's mum had been really worried, she had been crying and had to go and see his nana and granddad every day. Tom said he was sad because his mum was sad and busy and he did not know what was wrong with his granddad and his sister had been making tea and she does not make it properly, like his mum does.

Having heard what has been happening for Tom, what might the school do to support Tom and his family?

Families, social and cultural capital

We know from a range of research that a child's capacity to achieve at school, and therefore be in a better position to achieve long-term well-being, is hugely determined by the start in life provided by the child's family. In terms of ensuring a child has physical and emotional well-being, government research shows that 'the things that matter most are a healthy pregnancy; good maternal mental health; secure bonding with the child; love and responsiveness of parents' (Field 2010, p. 5). The same report states that 'by the age of three, a baby's brain is 80% formed and his or her experiences before then shape the way the brain has grown and developed' (ibid.). Similarly, early engagement with stimulating activities, both at home and in the local environment, and the chance to interact with a range of people provide good 'opportunities for a child's cognitive, language and social and emotional development' (ibid.). Just as children who have strong attachments develop the self-esteem and the confidence to try new things and be curious about life and learning, a child, even from a very young age, who has been engaged in stimulating activities is more likely to try new and possibly challenging activities in the EY setting and at school. One of the further draw-backs of thinking about families only in terms of the nuclear family model is that it tends to view families as isolated units when in effect few families operate in complete isolation. Families are linked to one another, to their wider community and to society at the broadest national, if not international, level.

Reflective activity

Figure 1.1 Who are my family?

Draw a circle and in it write the names of those you regard as being your closest family.

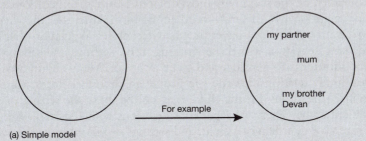

(a) Simple model

Think about how the families of those whose names you have put in the circle form part of your wider family.

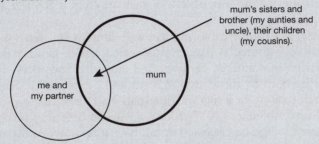

(b) Extended family model

Add more circles for each of your close family members. Who in their family do you feel are part of your wider family?

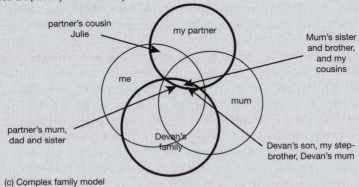

(c) Complex family model

Figure 1.1 Who are my family? Part (a) shows a simple family model; (b) shows an extended family model; and (c) shows a complex family model.

Very quickly we can see that trying to define the limits of what might be termed a family can be very messy to determine, particularly for someone outside a family group looking in. When you have made new friends, or as you have got to know a partner, trying to understand and remember who others regard as part of their family and the relationships within their family can be very complicated. And, as we have seen from our earlier reflective activity, often those who people feel they have the closest relationships with may not, to the outsider, be the seemingly most obvious family member. For example, someone might have both a birth mother and birth father that they live with, or who has brought them up, yet they may feel closer to an aunt, a sibling or even the lady next door. For those working in EY settings and schools, these are important ideas to consider and to be aware of. Many children will have complex family relationships and the people children feel closest to, or who are significant in caring for the child, may not be those the setting or school expect them to be. There are legal considerations with regard to who is the actual parent or guardian of a child, and settings or schools must be aware of these; however, on a day-to-day basis it is worth bearing in mind that when we say to children 'take this book home and read it with mum', it may be a sibling, an aunt or the lady next door that the child is actually going to read the book with.

A further reason for exploring the way families and relationships within families are constituted is that, as mentioned earlier, families do not live in isolation from one another. Families, and individual members of families, are impacted on both by those around them and by events happening at wider community, national or sometimes international levels. This is an idea explored by Urie Bronfenbrenner (1917–2005), a Russian American psychologist, and as a concept can best be discussed through what is known as Bronfenbrenner's ecological environment model (Figure 1.2). Bronfenbrenner's model explores how a child is surrounded by and grows up into a community, and how the child's interaction with the different 'layers' of that community will help shape aspects of who that child grows up to be, the experiences that they will have, the characteristics they develop and the opportunities that the child is provided with.

Bronfenbrenner's model is helpful to consider as it enables us to think about how children, even from the earliest age, are members of wider society, and their lives, again even from birth, are impacted on by what is happening in the society into which they are born and grow up. In this way we can see how the well-being of children, families and society is closely interlinked. If families thrive, children and society thrives. In considering these ideas it is also helpful to explore Maslow's theory of the hierarchy of needs and self-actualisation (Spohrer 2008). Figure 1.3 shows how Maslow explored the notion that in order to attain self-actualisation, or what we might term well-being, we need to have a range of needs met. As the diagram shows, at the bottom of the pyramid the most basic needs we have are such things as food, water, warmth, shelter and sleep. It is only when these needs are met, argued

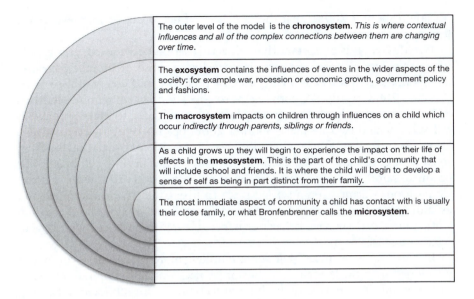

Figure 1.2 Bronfenbrenner's ecological environment model. Sources (Deater-Deckard 2004; Empson 2004; Knowles and Lander 2011).

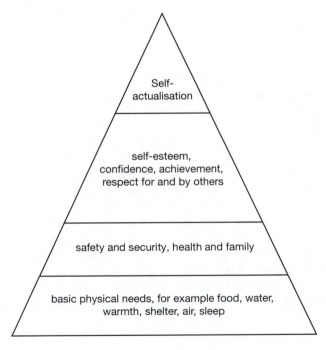

Figure 1.3 Maslow's theory of the hierarchy of needs and self-actualisation. Adapted from Spohrer (2008, p. 18).

Maslow (Spohrer 2008), that the next level of needs can be met, eventually leading to the achievement of well-being.

For Maslow, it is important that self-actualisation be achieved, as it is only when this happens that we can also develop 'a sense of morality, creativity, spontaneity, problem solving, lack of prejudice and acceptance of facts' (Spohrer 2008, p. 18). So, with regard to education, which requires children to be operating at level three in this hierarchy, 'we need to make sure needs at levels one and two are met' (Spohrer 2008, pp. 18–19). However, we also know that not all children and families live in social contexts that enable them to easily access many of the elements that support achieving well-being. For example, families living in poverty may not have access to the most nourishing food, warmth and a settled place to live. Children from refugee and asylum seeker families may be unsafe, dislocated and anxious, and children who are in care may have behaviour issues relating to problems with attachment and self-esteem.

In this way we can see that some families, more than others, are better positioned to provide for the higher-order needs of children and are therefore more likely to enable their children to be ready for school and learning and eventually to be able to reach self-actualisation. Families that have a greater capacity to provide for their children in this way are, to use Bourdieu's term, in possession of more social and cultural capital than other families (Carter 2005; Fine 2010). When we think of capital we usually think of it as referring to financial or economic capital – that is, to having a surplus of money once basic items such as food are bought, which can be used to buy particular goods and assets we want, such as houses – whereas social capital assets 'can be anything from your personal acquaintances (not what but who you know) and family, through communal or associational activity, to your identity or culture' (Fine 2010, p. ix). Not only do some families possess more social capital than others, they may also have more cultural capital too.

This complex issue of culture is discussed in more detail in the next chapter; however, in terms of Bourdieu's notion of cultural capital (Carter 2005) we are referring here to how society values such things as certain genres of music, art, books and even television programmes as being of more value than others. For example, classical music is often regarded as having more value than popular music; classic literature as being better than thrillers; and educational documentaries as more worthwhile to watch on the television than soap operas. This notion of cultural capital has also been linked to the notion of why some children achieve better at school than others. There is an argument that in the UK education is linked to a particular cultural focus and that children whose family culture is different from that of the school lack the knowledge and understanding, or cultural capital, to engage with what the school is offering.

Case study

Jerome and Kyle are 10-year-old boys. Jerome's dad is a doctor; Jerome lives in a detached house and has his own bedroom. He also has his own computer and games console. He plays the violin in a local youth orchestra and his parents often attend concerts the orchestra puts on. Jerome also plays football for a local youth team and his team is at the top of the local youth league's second division. Jerome's mother is worried that he is not doing well in maths so she has recently arranged for him to have a maths tutor. Jerome also has an older sister who is at university.

Kyle lives in a social housing flat; it is a ground floor flat, which is a necessity because his mum is in a wheelchair. Kyle's dad is a department manager in a local DIY store and works shifts, often having to work at the weekend, which means sometimes Kyle and his younger brother have to be there for their mum. Kyle shares a bedroom and has access to the family computer, which he and his brother also use to play games on. Kyle would like to play the guitar; however, his school does not offer any instrument lessons or have the facility to let children borrow instruments. He would also like to play football but cannot always get to the away games, so he is not a member of a team. Kyle struggles with his reading; his mum is keen to hear him read at home. To avoid having to read to his mum Kyle 'forgets' to bring books home from school, knowing that there is not much else to read at home.

Although this is a rather contrived example of how two children's lives can be different, it is deliberately like this to show how social and cultural capital operates. Read through the case study again and list those social advantages and cultural advantages Jerome has over Kyle; advantages that might give Jerome an added advantage in terms of achieving at school.

Children who grow up in families that can enable them to have access to a range of life experiences build up a repertoire of behaviours and a bank of knowledge and understanding that can build confidence and self-esteem. They learn that the world is full of different situations but they have a range of experiences they can draw on to help them deal with any new and unfamiliar situations that they may find themselves in. The broader the experiences a family can provide for a child, the greater the child's access to a range of social and cultural experiences and understanding, the higher the child's stores of social capital and the greater his or her likelihood of achieving in learning.

Educational achievement in the UK is in turn linked to what is known as social mobility. Social mobility is about being able to move from one social arena to another; it is usually associated with 'getting on', that is to say, getting a good education and qualifications that will lead to financially rewarding work and the capacity to buy such things as houses.

The role of the school in providing equality of opportunity for children to achieve

The research shows that the more social and cultural capital a child has, the more likely they are to achieve well at school. This notion of social and cultural capital is a concept that is discussed in the context of different families throughout this book. For those children who, for a variety of reasons, have more limited social and cultural capital it may be for the school to 'make up' the difference. Without recognising the impact of the notion of social and cultural capital it is likely that a child's access to social mobility and self-actualisation, through education, will be restricted. The research also shows that a child's social mobility through education can also be restricted where there is a tension between the values, attitudes and beliefs held by the school and those lived by at home. In this way, EY settings and schools need to ensure that they are 'connecting' with all the families that their children have and work with diverse families to ensure that they are not, however inadvertently, creating barriers to learning. To help success in this aim government research (Field 2010) shows that where children are achieving in their education it is where EY settings and schools are working *with* families to develop *shared notions* of a *positive parenting* approach that, in turn, enables the home, as a learning environment, to support achievement in education.

Conclusion

> Strong families give children love, identity, a personal history and a secure base from which to explore and enjoy life as they grow up. And families are where most of us find the support and care necessary for a happy and fulfilling life – as children and adults, parents and grandparents too.
>
> (DCSF 2010a, p. 1)

As we have explored in this chapter, and as the UK government states, 'families come in all shapes and sizes' and in terms of enabling a child to achieve at school it does not matter how a family is organised; what does matter is that there are 'stable and loving relationships between adults in the home – parents, grandparents and other caring adults' (ibid.). What also matters, in terms of educational achievement, is that EY settings and schools recognise what is working well for the child in terms of his or her family background and work with that to enable the child to achieve in their learning. This chapter has explored the main aspects of why family is important to long-term well-being and educational achievement. The next chapter further develops the notion of how families help develop individual identity and why this is an important concept to consider when thinking about educational achievement. The subsequent chapters explore in more detail some of the myriad ways that families may be constituted and aspects of these family unit settings that schools need to think about, thereby ensuring that their approaches to working with families connect as well as they can with all children's families.

2 Families, identity and cultural heritage

Gianna Knowles

This chapter explores:

- what is meant by identity and cultural heritage;
- the link between developing an individual identity and having social responsibility;
- the link between family, identity, culture and achieving in learning;
- identity, culture, race and ethnicity;
- teachers' standards; and
- gender, identity and learning.

Identity and cultural heritage

This chapter discusses the notion of identity and cultural heritage and why these concepts are important to consider in relation to better understanding how children might be enabled to achieve in their learning. Britain is a country that is diverse, both in the range of ways families can be organised and in terms of the cultural and ethnic heritage they may come from. Everyone has an ethnicity and many ethnic groups have a distinctive cultural dimension. Although it is acknowledged that the notion of culture can be difficult to define (Rosenthal and Barry 2009; Rai and Panna 2010), it is generally accepted that when we think about culture we are referring to those practices that are associated with the social aspect of people's lives. In particular, culture and what might be seen as cultural practices can relate to aspects of life involving 'marriage, sexuality, dress, diet, education, body marking, and funeral customs' (Rosenthal and Barry 2009, p. 229). That is to say, what unites many distinctive ethnic groups is that they have customs and practices around the social dimension of their lives: what they eat, wear, the role of men and women within the group and the nature and purpose of education.

Reflective activity

Culture is that complex whole which includes knowledge, belief, art, morals, law, custom and other capabilities and habits acquired by man as a member of society.

(Edward Taylor cited in Rai and Panna 2010, p. 3)

Culture includes all aspects of human activity from the fine arts to popular entertainment, from everyday behaviour to the development of sophisticated technology. It includes plans, rules, techniques, designs and policies for living . . . Every human group has a culture. It differs from society to society. It also has different origins, that is, it is marked by uniqueness.

(Rai and Panna 2010, p. 8)

What do you think of as being your dominant cultural beliefs and practices? Think about what you wear and what you eat, the festivals you celebrate and the music you listen to. Do you consider yourself as belonging to a specific ethnic group and having cultural practices that reflect that group? Thinking about more complex cultural beliefs, do your views on marriage, bringing up children, rules about right and wrong and the role of men and women in society reflect a particular cultural view?

Although some cultural values and practices can be seen as belonging to distinct groups of people, even within those groups there will be different opinions about what constitutes expression of that culture. There will also be hierarchies in terms of what are the better and more valuable expressions of those forms, compared with popular expressions of cultural forms. For example, if we consider dance as a form of cultural expression in Europe, classical ballet is usually regarded as the most valuable, 'highest' or most legitimate form of dance. By contrast, dance forms such as ballroom dancing, street dance, hip-hop and disco are regarded as having less value and being 'lower' forms of cultural expression. However, what can begin as being a 'popular' form of cultural expression can, over time, become legitimised. In the same way, one culture will absorb ideas and expressions of culture from other groups. In this way, the notion of culture, even cultural forms attributed to distinct groups, has the capacity to change and develop, particularly in diverse societies such as Britain. Further to this, in areas where there may be people who come from a range of cultural heritages, the distinctions between cultural practices from different groups often begin to overlap. Many people, if asked to think about it carefully, will talk about practices that they were taught as a child that are specific to their own cultural heritage; however, more often in the business of day-to-day life individuals will draw on ideas, beliefs and practices from a range of cultures depending on their own interests, attitudes and values. There is also a notion that it is important to preserve the distinctions between the cultures of different societal groups. Some people are concerned by what they see as important aspects of their own culture being eroded and lost under the influence of others' cultures. However, these tensions are more often inter-generational than cross-cultural. Cultures change because the next generation generates new expressions of culture, not necessarily because one culture has swamped another.

Case study

Morwenna is 73 years old. She says:

> When I was a child I wanted to be a teacher but my parents believed it would be a waste of money to educate a girl beyond 16, they thought the role of a woman was to get married and keep home. So that is what I did. I felt quite resentful that my younger brother could stay on at school. When my girls were born I made quite sure they would have a better education than me and make more of the opportunities available to them. Of course, in many ways it was easier for them to do this as society's attitudes had changed by the time they were 16 too.

Morwenna's daughter is 50 years old. She says:

> From an early age I knew I was expected to go to University and get a good job. I know why mum wanted me to do this, but sometimes I think it was more about her than me – half of me is from my dad, after all. Sometimes I think she saw only the opportunities she thought she had missed, not the hard work of getting qualifications, getting a job and later deciding what to do about being a mother and working or not working. We used to have big battles about what I could do as a teenager – going out, having boyfriends. I know she was scared I would throw away my chance at what she saw as freedom, but I wanted to be doing what my friends were doing.

Morwenna's granddaughter is 16 years old. She says:

> My grandmother grew up in a very rural part of the UK where every-one was the same and your whole future was almost organised before you were born. I have been brought up in a big city and I am used to there being all sorts of different people around me. I can see that there are many ways to live your life. I have friends who come from families completely different to mine. We sort of know this about each other, but it doesn't make a difference as we are just friends and get on with those things we want to do together and think about the same as each other. I have Muslim friends who I swap presents with at Christmas and I have been invited round to their houses at Eid and to celebrate the end of Ramadan with them.

Cultural attitudes, values, beliefs and practices give groups a sense of identity and individuals within those groups a sense of belonging. We are not born having a culture; it is something we learn about as we grow up. Therefore what we describe as being 'our culture' will depend on what we have been taught it should be.

Identity

There is considerable disagreement over what the term 'identity' might mean and how identities are formed. There is also disagreement about just how important the notion of identity is in debates relating to success in learning. However, in terms of achievement, we are concerned with identity for three reasons, all of which we will begin to explore in this chapter and come back to in subsequent chapters in this book. First of all, in Europe and North America there is a widespread belief that to flourish as human beings we need to have 'a sense of self', to know 'who we are'. Second, having a sense of who we are engenders a sense of belonging and security. That is, we can relate to and belong with others who share the values, attitudes and beliefs we hold; we can share in a wider cultural identity, which will also give us a sense of history and of being related to something of value that goes back in time and will continue forward. Third, if we know who we are, we also know who we are not. That is, just as we can derive security from identifying with groups of others and established cultural forms, so too we know who we are not like and do not want to associate with, or be associated with.

One of the first notions relating to identity to explore is: to what extent is our identity because of our genetic inheritance, or developed in response to influences around us? As noted above, sometimes identity is discussed in terms of everyone having a true self that can flourish only under particular circumstances, similar to Maslow's notion of self-actualisation discussed earlier. Many will agree that although we can often seem to change or modify aspects of our character and physical appearance, for a variety of reasons, fundamentally there remains an unchanging part of us, which is our true identity (Garrett 1998).

Reflective activity

Having considered the broader notion of the cultural attitudes, values and practices you feel you have, think about how you have shaped these, or have been shaped by them, to develop what you would see as being your own identity.

Do you feel that your culture influences what you eat and what you wear, but that in certain ways the way you dress and the food you eat is particular to you and specific choices you make about these things? It may be that you would dress in a particular way for particular reasons and eat certain foods at particular times – festival times, for example. Yet outside these special circumstances you have a distinct personal identity and do things in more general ways to suit your lifestyle.

You may also have found that as you gain more life experience and come into contact with a wider range of cultures, attitudes and beliefs, that aspects of what you would call your identity have changed and developed in response to these experiences.

In much of Europe and North America the contemporary notion of this idea of a central *self* owes much to the work of Sigmund Freud. Freud began to develop his ideas at the end of the nineteenth century. He introduced the now familiar notion that we develop our sense of self, particularly in terms of our behaviours, beliefs, values and attitudes, as a result of how we have learnt, since we were infants, to respond to and manage the social environment around us (Rennison 2001). From Freud's initial work have evolved discussions about to what extent we are simply products of those environments and to what extent we have control over how we manage the influences around us and choose, either consciously or unconsciously, which ones we allow to become part of our identity and which ones we want to reject. In other words, how much of who we believe ourselves to be and others see us as being is because of nurture, how and where we have been brought up, or nature, the genetic 'blue-print' we have inherited from our families (Lawler 2009)?

Individual identity and social responsibility

In the previous chapter we explored Maslow's notion that it is important for human beings to be able to achieve self-actualisation, or fulfilment of potential (Spohrer 2008). For a life to be 'well-lived' or to be a 'meaningful life' (Robinson 2007, p. 16) and one of value, human beings need access to certain goods and experiences such as education, friendship and experiences that build self-esteem as well as those things needed for basic survival. Education is often seen as something that is important in terms of giving life value and in making life more meaningful. In his hierarchy of needs Maslow includes, as being necessary to achieving self-actualisation, safety, health, family and relationships. Towards the top of his list of what is needed for self-actualisation he also cites confidence, personal achievements and gaining respect from others. That is to say, in terms of developing, as part of their identity, self-esteem and confidence in their ability to succeed and achieve, children need environments that allow this to happen for them, both in the home and at school.

The United Nations Universal Declaration of Human Rights (www. un.org) also recognises the importance of personal identity and the need for human beings to have the opportunity to develop that identity. The UN Declaration of Human Rights is written up as 30 articles, or statements, outlining what amounts to the minimum entitlements all human beings should expect to be in place. These entitlements that will enable all to live a meaningful life follow much of what we have already discussed in relation to Maslow's hierarchy of needs. The first set of articles state that all human beings have a right to be recognised as being of value and that each individual is as important as any other human being, and that all human beings should be allowed liberty and be treated fairly and justly, while article 22 states: 'Everyone, as a member of society, has the right to . . . realization . . . of the economic, social and cultural rights indispensable for his dignity and the free development of his personality' (www.un.org).

Reflective activity

The American Declaration of Independence, signed in 1776, states that the rights we hold by virtue of being human include the right to 'Life, Liberty and the pursuit of Happiness' (www.archives.gov).

Other conventions and legislation that uphold human rights echo those outlined in the American Declaration of Independence. For example, both the United Nations Universal Declaration of Human Rights and the UK's Human Rights Act 1998 (www.legislation.gov.uk/ ukpga/1998/42/contents) contain rights that uphold the right to life, liberty, freedom of speech and freedom of expression.

Rights such as the right to meet with and associate with who we wish, to pursue activities and ideas that interest us, to be part of a religion of our own choosing and to marry who we wish are also rights under UK law (www.legislation.gov.uk/) and the UN convention (www.un.org).

However, it is only the American Declaration of Independence that mentions the notion of 'happiness'.

What does the term 'identity' mean to you? How is the notion of your identity, who you feel you are, linked to notions of pursuing your own happiness, having freedom to go where you want, choose work that interests you, follow a religion of your own choice, or not, and form relationships with people of your own choosing?

How free have your choices been? Are they influenced by other factors around you? Do you feel you have a duty to limit what you do as it may impact on the lives of others?

One of the reasons the notion of identity, self-actualisation or the 'development of personality' is considered so important is because of the idea of moral agency or autonomy. For example, if we consider the notion of happiness as outlined in the American Declaration of Independence, currently it could be argued there is a tendency to think of happiness as the pursuit of 'individual will and private interest' (Malloch *et al.* 2006, p. viii); that is, the pursuit of personal happiness is often easily confused with the pursuit of pleasure, in whatever way the individual chooses to define it. However, with regard to the notion of the pursuit of happiness in the Declaration of Independence, Malloch argues that what Thomas Jefferson meant was not 'personal pleasure' but that 'the pursuit of truth was the highest form of his pursuit of happiness' (Malloch *et al.* 2006, p. viii). That is, the notion of happiness used here is one that is about an 'activation and engagement of all the appetites, desires, and capacities that make up a person in a balanced, well-adapted way' (Malloch *et al.* 2006, p. 8).

Therefore, identity can be seen as being the pursuit of personal wants and possibly pleasures under the guise of exercising our rights to achieve self-actualisation. Or it can be seen as being about having a strong sense of self that we have developed through reflecting on ideas. It is about exercising our rights responsibly, considering experiences we have been through, and finding ways to develop an approach to living in a complex society that benefits both ourselves and others. This does not mean to say that we might not do things simply because they give us pleasure, but that we recognise we live as members of a society in which our actions can impact for good or for harm on others.

This notion of being able to reflect on and control who we are and possibly, who we want to be is known as 'reflexivity' (Chambers 2001, p. 20). In early years (EY) settings and schools the activities we undertake with children often encourage them to develop reflective skills; we read stories to them that give examples of characters behaving in particular ways and we ask children to think about the good and bad in those situations, usually guiding them to behave in the ways that we think of as being good. We reward and praise behaviours and actions we want to encourage children to engage in and we seek to give them confidence and self-esteem, as we know that, not only will they then be happier in their learning, but they will also progress in their learning. In this way, we have a direct impact on how children's sense of self and identity develops. Indeed, there is a very strong view held by much of wider society that this is one of the prime functions of education.

Reflective activity

In June 2011 the government's Minister for Education stated that:

> lives can be transformed by what goes on in schools. The precious moments spent in the classroom, the interactions between professionals and students, the process of teaching and learning – can shape futures like nothing else . . . Introducing the next generation to the best that has been thought and written is a moral enterprise of which we can all be proud. Giving every child an equal share in the inheritance of achievement which great minds have passed on to us is a great progressive cause . . . Because it is only through learning – the acquisition of intellectual capital – that individuals have the power to shape their own lives.
>
> (Gove 2011)

Do you agree with this analysis of what education can do and should do? What subjects and skills do you think children need to be engaged with in schools to ensure that they 'have the power to shape their own lives?' (ibid.).

Currently we find in the UK a wide acceptance of the notion that we have a right to pursue ways of living and expressing ourselves that meet our own personal needs and desires. This approach to life, combined with cultural diversity and access to liberating technologies that introduce us to new ideas and different ways of living, can, as Chambers (2001) suggests, lead to a situation in which 'concepts of the self and family are therefore being redefined. Individuals are now experimenting in new living arrangements in the absence of old certainties and binding values' (Chambers 2001, p. 20).

Family identity, culture and school

Education happens in the social realm. That is to say, usually what happens in EY settings and schools is managed by a group of people who have their own ideas about what children should be engaged in. However, education is also impacted on by wider societal values. Some of education is controlled by nationally agreed ideas and most of education is regulated through an inspection process to ensure it is deemed, by wider societal values, effective. In this way, most of what happens in schools and impacts on children's development, including their developing identity and sense of self, happens in public and is, therefore, subject to regulation. We also know that much of what influences children in terms of their behaviour, values, attitudes and identity will have been developed by their family background. In a vast majority of instances there is synchronicity between values, attitudes, behaviours and general beliefs between home and places of education, but not always. One of the challenges for EY settings and primary schools is to ensure that the learning environment they are providing is welcoming, secure and motivates the interests of the learner. Part of the challenge in achieving such an environment is the partnerships that EY settings and schools develop with the families of the children they work with.

Notions of identity and culture are becoming increasingly understood in terms of the way identity and culture relate to educational achievement. As we have discussed, children develop an identity within a frame of cultural references. Further to this, often our identities are shaped by our sense of a need to belong. Part of being who we are is who we identify with: usually those who share similar values, attitudes and beliefs to those we hold. As Weedon (2004, p. 1) states: 'Identity is about belonging, about what you have in common with some people and what differentiates you from others'. And, just as children come into educational settings with an identity and cultural heritage, so too do the adults who work with them. Data on pupil achievement over the past 10 years have shown that children from particular sectors of society have consistently underachieved. Those children who are underachieving are children from particular ethnic groups, classes and genders, namely, black boys from African-Caribbean backgrounds, children from Pakistani and Bangladeshi backgrounds and white working-class boys. Children from Chinese and white Asian backgrounds, however, do better than all pupils (Gilborne and Mirza 2000; DCSF 2010b; Knowles and Lander 2011). And the most recent GCSE attainment figures show that of children with English as an additional language (EAL):

> 80.8 per cent of EAL pupils achieved five A*–C GCSEs last year, compared with 80.4 per cent of pupils with English as their mother tongue. Native English speakers are still slightly ahead on the five A*–C GCSEs including English and maths benchmark. But EAL pupils have steadily closed the gap on the measure since 2008.
>
> (TES 2012)

For children with EAL, who are doing so well in their English achievement, it is suggested that their success is because of 'the drive and aspiration of immigrant families, combined with the educational boost provided by fluency in more than language' (ibid.). Just to complicate the picture further, although data show that ethnicity is a factor that must be considered in looking at the overall picture of educational achievement and underachievement, so too is the need to consider other factors such as gender, since attainment data also show that some girls are consistently outperforming some boys in certain subjects.

Although complex, what the achievement data and follow-up research do tell us is that children are more likely to succeed if they feel they can identify with and belong to the culture and cultures promoted by the school. In this way, it is also understood that if a child comes into a school that has a culture and practices they cannot identify with, it may be that the child will fail to thrive and achieve in their learning. As Knowles and Lander (2011, p. 8) state:

> where individuals or organisations transmit messages that suggest only particular aspects of certain cultures are acknowledged and others are ignored or marginalised . . . it can marginalise children and erode their sense of self, or who they identify themselves as being.

Mismatches between home and school culture happen for a variety of reasons. Sometimes it is because a child's ethnicity and culture is not apparent in the school they attend and therefore the child feels alienated in their school surroundings. Sometimes the differences in culture are not to do with ethnicity, but for reasons of social class. Brannen and colleagues (2000) also explore how similar tensions can occur for children across a range of institutions that they may come into contact with since 'children's childhoods are also shaped by processes of institutionalisation' (Brannen *et al*. 2000, p. 6), for example, being a child in care, a child who is fostered or one who has come to this country seeking asylum. Such issues are discussed in more detail in later chapters in this book.

Reflective activity

Human beings have an infinite capacity for taking on board new ideas and adapting to new situations. Children new to an EY setting or school will encounter ideas, experiences and values that they may not have come across before. Most EY settings and schools recognise that in these situations children will go through a time of transition and will need support in making that transition.

Connecting with the child and family

Think about what is good practice in supporting children through such transitions. What have you seen in terms of schools working with families to help develop a partnership between the school and family? How do good partnerships ensure children know what to expect from being in an EY setting or school?

Before starting in a new EY setting or school, children need to visit and look around. Children want to know where they need to go to when they arrive, where they put their coat, where the toilet is, who the people are around them and where they will eat their lunch.

A visit to home from the EY setting or school also helps make the link between home and school. It can be an opportunity to talk about what the child is interested in and chat about what the family would like to help support the child's learning

Coming in to a setting or school that reflects how things happen at home will also enable a child to feel more settled. If the pictures on the walls, the books in the book corner and the play activities are those which the child can relate to in terms of their cultural references, then the child will feel that the things around them are familiar and that they understand what people expect of them in this new context.

Identity, culture, race and ethnicity

Ensuring that children feel their identities and cultures are acknowledged in the EY settings and schools they attend not only enables them to better access learning activities, but is also necessary to address issues of racism and discrimination. All EY settings and schools are very aware of the need to tackle deliberate racism and discrimination; however, what they sometimes find harder to address is unwitting discrimination that can arise through lack of thought for, or understanding of, how they may be marginalising the culture of some of the children they work with.

Case study

As a student teacher on a school experience in south London, Karen was asked to teach a maths lesson about graphs to a Year 2 class. She decided to ask the children to collect and graph data about their favourite foods. She prepared a data collection sheet containing a list of what she assumed would be the children's favourite foods. On the list was pizza, fish and chips, burgers and ice cream. The lesson did not go as well as she had expected. When she discussed it with her class teacher the teacher said: ask the children to write their own list of favourite foods and then collect the data to graph. The second lesson went much better; it transpired the children's favourite foods were curried goat and jerk chicken. Few, if any, of the class ate pizza.

Reflective activity

Early years settings and schools have a duty not only to connect with the different cultures children in their schools come from to ensure individual children can achieve, but also to promote children's understanding of the range of cultures that constitute UK society. The Office for Standards in Education, Children's Services and Skills (OfSTED 2004) discusses how children need to have knowledge and understanding about their own and others' cultures.

> Cultural development is about pupils' . . . feeling comfortable in a variety of cultures and being able to operate in the emerging world culture of shared experiences provided by television, travel and the internet. It is about understanding that cultures are always changing and coping with change. Promoting pupils' cultural development is intimately linked with schools' attempts to value cultural diversity and prevent racism.
>
> (OfSTED 2004, p. 23)

Examples of good practice

Children need to be in a learning environment that enables them to develop an understanding of their own culture as this gives children a sense of identity and a language with which to communicate (ibid.).

Children need to develop cultural understanding that involves knowing about the customs of particular cultures as well as elements of that culture's history, geography, icons and images, artefacts, music, painting, sculpture, dance and technology (ibid.). However, this needs to happen in a way that goes beyond the simply tokenistic.

Children need to experience culture as something vibrant and dynamic and understand that ideas and practices, in all cultures, change and develop.

An educational setting that reflects the cultural diversity of the UK is one that enables children to:

- recognise and understand their own cultural assumptions and values
- appreciate cultural diversity and accord dignity and respect to other people's values and beliefs

- achieve a sense of personal enrichment through encounter with cultural media and traditions from a range of cultures
- develop a regard for the heights of human achievement in all cultures and societies and
- an appreciation of the diversity and interdependence of cultures.

(OfSTED 2004, p. 25)

Teachers' standards

From September 2012 the Department for Education is introducing new teacher standards which those teaching in the UK need to adhere to as part of their professional duty. The new standards will apply to all teachers regardless of their career stage, and define the minimum level of practice expected of teachers from the point of being awarded qualified teacher status (QTS) onwards (DfE 2011, p. 2). The standards cover aspects of teachers' personal and professional conduct and 'set the required standard for conduct throughout a teacher's career' (ibid., p. 9). The standards require that teachers show 'tolerance of and respect for the rights of others' (ibid.). They are also expected not to undermine 'fundamental British values, including democracy, the rule of law, individual liberty and mutual respect, and tolerance of those with different faiths and beliefs' (ibid.). Although framed, in this context, as 'fundamental British values' (ibid.), many cultures and indeed nation states see as being fundamental to their values the notions and pursuit of 'democracy, the rule of law, individual liberty and mutual respect, and tolerance' (ibid.).

Gender, identity and learning

We have spent most of this chapter exploring how children come to understand themselves in terms of their identity and the impact of their cultural heritage on identity. As briefly mentioned earlier, cultural heritage is not only about ethnicity; it also includes the notion of social class. Social class is discussed in more detail in Chapter 10. However, before we finish this initial discussion about identity, culture, home school relationships and learning we do need to give some consideration to the notion of gender, identity and cultural heritage. Gender is important in our discussion about identity and culture, as gender is another of the constitutions that we need to take into account when we are thinking about achievement and underachievement. As discussed earlier, in some areas of learning the achievement of girls seems to be outperforming that of boys; for example, at Key Stages 1 and 2, and in some GCSEs, girls are achieving better than boys in reading and writing in English (DCSF 2009a; OfSTED 2003, 2007, 2011). However, we need to be careful when we think about how this information might impact on the learning activities we provide, since not *all* girls are outperforming *all* boys.

At birth, usually depending on primary sex characteristics, children are normally determined as being boys or girls, male or female. However, although male and female can be termed biological distinctions, many argue that we have control over how we manifest our *gender*, particularly in terms of our behaviours, attitudes, values and beliefs. When identifying our gender we may say we are male, female or transgender, and there is considerable argument over whether the way we manifest that gender is genetic or learnt behaviour. As Fausto-Sterling (2000) discusses, sometimes not only are there instances where there is ambiguity about the primary sex characteristics that are present at birth, where 'scientists, medical professionals, and the wider public have made sense of (or ought to make sense of) bodies that present themselves as neither entirely male nor entirely female' (Fausto-Sterling 2000, p. 3), but also there is more to being male or female than the physical characteristics of the body. That is to say: 'labeling someone a man or a woman is a social decision. We may use scientific knowledge to help us make the decision, but only our beliefs about gender – not science – can define our sex' (ibid.). Therefore, some writers argue (Burr 1998; Fausto-Sterling 2000; Riger 2000) that, biology aside, society constructs ideas about how girls and boys, men and woman should behave and what their role in society should be. What we understand about how 'our genders' should behave we learn through 'advertisements, toys, newspaper debates, "men's lifestyle" magazines, the classroom, the school, psychiatric interviews, language textbooks, a party, poetry and parentcraft texts' (Litosseliti and Sunderland 2002, p. 1).

In this way, we can see how children can be taught that to be a girl means to behave in particular ways, and similarly boys can learn what it is to be a boy. Not only does society, in the widest sense, through national and international media, project certain messages about gender roles, but individual cultural groups will also have their own gendered roles within the larger picture. In this way, the groups children identify with will also impact on how they perform their gender and, in turn, this may impact on how they approach learning. For example, if children are brought up to identify with female roles that see women as being subservient and not needing education they will carry that belief into school. In the same way, if boys identify with groups who do not see it as being masculine to learn and study, they too will underachieve. Early years settings and schools need to be very aware of how the children they work with are building their gender identities and how that may impact on their understanding of learning as part of their gender and identity. Enabling both boys and girls to achieve may require more than simply ensuring all children have access to a range of gender-neutral learning activities; it may require those managing the learning environment to actively counteract negative gender identification.

Throughout this chapter we have discussed a range of complex ideas that have sought to raise our awareness about individual and family identity and culture. We have also begun to explore how these aspects of children's lives impact on how children relate to different learning environments. We will return to many of the ideas introduced here throughout the rest of the book.

However, before we move on to consider some of these issues in more detail, work through the activity below. This final activity for this chapter is designed to help you reflect on what you have just read and to ask you to further reflect on and consider what you mean by 'family', before we move on to look at particular family groupings in more depth.

Reflective activity

This activity enables you to explore what it means to hold particular attitudes and beliefs in relation to the things you value. Since this is a book concerned with exploring family, the nature of what is meant by family and the different ways families can be constituted, we will take the notion of family to be the value we are exploring. First, give three reasons, at least, why you believe families to be of value. What is it that is special about families as a concept that you would not want to see lost and that you would be prepared to defend?

Often it is when we consider the notion of adoption that our values, attitudes and beliefs about what families are for and how they should be constituted are really tested. The comments below outline current tensions and procedures surrounding the issue of adoption in the UK. As you read them think about how the comments help you better understand what you believe is important about families.

> Latest government statistics show children wait an average of two years and seven months before being adopted, while this process takes more than three years in a quarter of cases. Potentially suitable adoptive parents are often turned away because they may not be the right ethnic match, are overweight or may have smoked.
>
> (Davies 2011)

> No citizen has a right to adopt. Children who have been placed with the wrong people, whose adoptions have broken down, and who have come back into the care system a second time, teach us that the assessment process has to be robust.
>
> (Douglas 2011)

> Adoption agencies responsible for placing children with their new families look for adopters from all walks of life. Gender, marital status, disability and employment status will not automatically exclude you from adopting a child. What matters most is your

ability to provide a permanent, caring and stable home, to meet the needs of a child from the care system.

(www.adoptionuk.org)

A mother has spoken of her anger that her two young children have been taken from the care of their grandparents and adopted by a homosexual couple.

(Cramb 2009)

Children raised by same-sex parents are being 'harmed'
(*Daily Mail* 2012, from a headline about Rick Santorum, an American Republican presidential candidate)

Advice for children about to be adopted on the Nottinghamshire County Council web-site:

In England and Wales **hundreds** of children are adopted every year. Like you, they are all children who for various reasons have not been able to live with their birth parents, so need a new family to **take care of them** until they are adults themselves. **What does being adopted mean?** Being adopted might sound really scary! . . . **Don't be afraid to ask!** The law says you are the most important person of all when you are going to be adopted, and everyone will want to **help you** as much as they can. **How do we find adoptive parents?** It takes a long time to decide whether adults will make **good adopters.**

(www.nottinghamshire.gov.uk)

3   Mixed race families

Radhika Holmström

This chapter explores:

* how the 'mixed race' category is a fast-growing ethnic group in the UK today;
* the stereotypes and assumptions about mixed race children, their families and their educational attainments;
* the conflation of 'mixed race' into 'black/Asian', and the limitations of this;
* the challenges for families that fall into the broad category of mixed race;
* being mixed race and the search for identity; and
* assumptions that can be made about mixed race families and children – for example identity confusion for children whose appearance does not reflect the complexity of their family background and whom others fail to connect with their culture.

Mixed race families

Why select 'mixed race' families specifically? Why not focus on 'black and minority ethnic' (BME) families, incorporating the area of mixed race within this? What is there about 'mixed race' that needs a chapter of its own? Does the vast range of families made up of parents from different countries and cultures have enough in common to make it possible to generalise?

This chapter looks at mixed race families, and some of the issues that early years (EY) practitioners and primary school teachers need to think about, precisely because mixed race issues often either get subsumed into the bigger area of BME families or are ignored because families vary so widely and it seems difficult to say anything meaningful. Over the past few decades, and particularly in this century, the topic of 'mixed race' has come much more to the fore; both from an academic and educational practitioner point of view, and from people of mixed ethnic origin themselves.

That this is so is because there are, in fact, some common themes spanning the whole range of mixed race families that apply to the 'mixed' experience, but also because there are some common *assumptions* made by other people about how mixed race families 'must' operate, and/or mixed race children 'must' feel or look. There is a whole range of clichés about mixed race families: notably the stereotype of the single-parent family of a white working-class mother who has been deserted by her black boyfriend. There is still a very common assumption that children whose parents come from different places, and/or children who have one black and one white parent, will be lonely and confused about their own identity and place in the world. And at the same time there is a stereotype of mixed race appearance, which may well be very physically attractive, but is also very prescriptive – not everyone of mixed ethnic origin looks the way they are 'supposed' to.

Mixed race families do, each time, have to work it out for themselves: how they are going to negotiate the mix of origins and cultures. And for most of those families, being of mixed origin is a positive thing; it is how other people perceive their family that can, potentially, make it negative.

Reflective activity

Here are some of the things that people say about mixed race children. How many of them do you recognise or agree with?

'Mixed race children are always very beautiful.'
'I don't agree with mixing – surely the children are always terribly confused.'
'Mixed race children aren't one or the other – they're neither black nor white. This must be very upsetting.'
'Mixed race children aren't one or the other – they're neither black nor white. They get the best of both worlds.'
'It's pointless talking about "mixed race" – these are black children, who are going to be treated as black children in a racist society.'
'It's hard to make a relationship work out between adults from such different cultures.'
'White women with black children are always going to find it hard to understand their children's heritage.'

Overall, do you think of 'mixed race' as a positive, or a negative?

How the 'mixed race' category is a fast-growing ethnic group in the UK today

Yet in spite of its growing importance in demographic terms and its entry into 'official' data collection, relatively little is known about the life experiences of so-called 'mixed' people, or how this new population grouping identifies in ethnic and racial terms – information which is crucial for our understandings of cultural diversity and the delivery of culturally competent public services. Important research (both in the USA and Britain) has debunked historical depictions of 'mixed' people as fragmented, marginal, and necessarily confused. Recent qualitative studies have demonstrated that 'mixed' people can and do make choices about their ethnic and racial identities (within structured parameters of 'choice'), but there is a multiplicity of views (both academic and popular) about what the growth of 'mixed' relationships and people augurs.

(Mai Sims 2007, p. 5)

'Mixed race', as opposed to 'other', was first used as an ethnic category in the UK census of 2001; however, this group of people has been growing steadily (in the UK and elsewhere) over the past 50 years. In fact, there have been people of mixed ethnic origin scattered around the UK for centuries: certainly dating back to the time of Roman soldiers (some of whom seem, on good archaeological evidence, to have been black). By 1788, Philip Thicknesse was complaining that 'in almost every village are to be seen a little race of mulattoes, mischievous as monkeys and infinitely more dangerous'. During the eighteenth and nineteenth centuries plenty of soldiers and traders in different parts of the British Empire fathered mixed race children, some of whom were sent, or brought back, to England.

There is not the same long-standing community of people of mixed race here as there has been in some other countries, such as South Africa's 'coloured' or India's Anglo-Indian populations; however, by the 1920s there were settled mixed race populations in a number of British seaports, including Liverpool and Cardiff (brought about in part by visiting African and Asian seamen) and significant communities in other cities including London and Manchester.

Importantly, many of the 'black' figures children learn about in school were in fact mixed race, including Mary Seacole and Bob Marley. Conversely, many 'white' people have black or Asian family too: from the footballer Ryan Giggs to the actor Alistair McGowan. There are a lot more mixed race people around than is perhaps acknowledged.

Today, the population of mixed race people in the UK is approaching a million, according to figures released by the Office of National Statistics (2011): from 672,000 in 2001 to 986,600 in 2009, which is an increase of nearly 50 per cent (Rogers 2011). A third are mixed Afro-Caribbean and white, followed by Asian/white. In age terms, a large proportion are children and young people; in the 2001 census, 17 per cent of the 'mixed' population was aged five or under.

This means that, in some schools and other EY settings today, a large proportion of children will have parents from different countries. In others, though, mixed raced children will be a rare minority, just as other ethnic minority children are. The highest proportion is in inner London; the lowest in the Scilly Isles, where the 2011 data showed no people of mixed race at all.

Case study

Aziz, Leonie and Yasmin are all in the reception class of an inner-city school.

Aziz's mother is from Pakistan, and his father is half Japanese and half Welsh. His parents divorced when he was very small, and he now lives with his father and his father's new (white) partner, with some contact with his mother. When he was born, his parents agreed to bring him up with some broadly Muslim rules (such as not eating pork) and his father still abides by this. Aziz does not really think about being mixed race – not least because there are a lot of other children in the school, such as his best friend, who are of similar origins.

Leonie's father is black British and her mother is white British. Her parents were born and brought up in the local area, and she has a lot of extended family on both sides living close by: she has white cousins, black cousins and also other mixed race cousins, since one of her mother's brothers is also married to a black woman. She thinks of herself as 'mixed' when she thinks about it all, but takes the shape of her family entirely for granted, including her white grandparents and her black grandparents.

Yasmin's parents met at medical school. Her father is originally from Nigeria, although he has lived in England since he was five, and her mother is white British. She tends to think of herself as white more than black: partly because she is very fair-skinned and partly because her parents do not have any particularly Nigerian connections or traditions in the house. At the same time, she recognises that her parents look different and that she has some African relatives, and she's looking forward to going to Nigeria and meeting more of them at some point.

The terminology: how we think about 'race'

The term 'mixed race', and indeed many other terms to do with race, make a lot of people (especially white people who do not usually have to think about race much) feel extremely uncomfortable. Race and colour are extremely loaded topics for most of us, and the terminology fluctuates too, ranging from the quasi-scientific, such as 'Caucasian', to terms that are essentially just a description of skin colour: white or black. The whole expression 'mixed race' is in its own way even more dubious, because it is again quasi-scientific without actually meaning much. Others prefer terms such as 'dual heritage', avoiding the associations with colour and physical appearance.

'I use the term mixed race because I think it's about the racialisation process,' says Dr Chamion Caballero, who is mixed race herself and specialises in this issue of parenting and families of mixed race. 'Everyone has mixed heritage or parenting, but if you have for example a white French mother and white British father your mixed heritage is perceived in a very different way' (interview with Caballero, 1 December 2011). Race is very often thought of as something you can spot, worn on the outside. Race discrimination is discrimination on the basis of colour as much as, or often more than, anything else. And this has a lot of different impacts on mixed race children, including children who might not initially be thought of as mixed race (see the section on mixed race children who do not look obviously 'black').

For instance the organisation MixD, which works with young mixed race people, says:

> The popular view of Mixed-Race is when your parents are of different racial backgrounds, usually some mixture of Black, Asian and White.
>
> Academics refer to someone being of Mixed-Race when she or he is a descendant of two or more groups currently believed to constitute distinct racial groups.
>
> A person with a White English Father and White French mother, it can be said has a mixed-culture or mixed-heritage but is not mixed-race; due to the fact that both parents come from the same racial group.
>
> (www.mix-d.org)

In practical terms, children with two white parents from different countries *are* likely to share some of the other issues common to children with one white and one non-white parent; however, as Caballero points out, they will not be subjected to the same assumptions as children who fall into the conventional category of mixed race. It is also important to remember that some children's mixed ethnic origins are very different from the more widespread white/black and white/Asian ones. They may have, for example:

- a Malay Chinese father and white British mother;
- a Spanish mother and a Mexican father; or
- a Japanese mother and a French father;

or, indeed, they may have two parents who are themselves of mixed ethnic origin.

Case study

Laila's parents are both Asian/white: her mother's mother is Indian and her father's father was from Bangladesh. Her parents were both brought up partly in Asia and partly in England: they both went to university in England and now work in 'professional' jobs.

Much of Laila's world is quite English – for example her parents both only speak English; however, there are a lot of Asian influences in her day-to-day life. Most of the pictures around the house are from India or Bangladesh and, although neither parent is religious, they have some small statues of Hindu gods and the Buddha, as well as a copy of the Koran on the bookshelf. Laila may get spaghetti bolognese or rice with kheema for tea.

Laila takes the whole mix of her parents' origins for granted. She thinks of her parents as mixed race and herself as mixed race. As far as she is concerned, having different relatives around the world is totally normal.

Expectations and assumptions: schooling

There is surprisingly little research into the educational achievements of this group of children. The data that do exist, however, show a wide divergence in the expectations of how well these children are going to do. White/black Caribbean pupils are both the largest group of mixed heritage pupils and the group most at risk of underachieving, in both primary and secondary school; white/black African pupils' attainment is close to average in primary and secondary school; and white/Asian pupils' attainment is above average. This is partly linked to other factors (such as levels of deprivation), but that is not the full picture.

The latest national statistics on Key Stage 1 attainment produced by the Department for Education and released on 11 November 2010 show that:

- Girls continue to outperform boys in all 4 elements (reading, writing mathematics and science) at Key Stage 1, with the biggest differences in reading and writing.
- Pupils of Indian, Chinese and Mixed White and Asian origin had the highest proportions achieving the expected level in reading, writing and mathematics. In science, a higher proportion of pupils from Mixed White and Asian, Indian and White British backgrounds achieved the expected level than their peers.
- A higher proportion of pupils whose first language is English achieved the expected level in all 4 elements than pupils for whom English is not their first language.
- Pupils not eligible for free school meals continue to outperform pupils known to be eligible for free school meals across all four elements. The gap is largest in reading and writing.
- Pupils resident in the least deprived areas, as defined by the Income Deprivation Affecting Children Index (IDACI), continue to

outperform pupils resident in the most deprived areas. The gap is largest in writing and smallest in mathematics.
(www.education.gov.uk/rsgateway/DB/SFR/s000968/index.shtml)

The research that does exist into why children from mixed white/black Caribbean families underachieve shows that schools do not particularly think about the *mix* as an issue.

> We found that whilst school policy statements expressed a commitment to tackle discrimination, racism and underachievement, these phenomena were expressed in 'mono heritage' terms that did not acknowledge the existence of mixed heritage pupils in the school or the specific barriers to learning faced by White/Black Caribbean learners.
>
> (Mai Sims 2007, p. 15)

Expectations and assumptions: background

Caballero and Edwards (2010, p. 3) have discussed how 'a number of methodologically dubious but influential research studies' conducted in the early twentieth century 'on racial mixing in Liverpool and Cardiff painted highly negative pictures of the families involved, stigmatizing the parents as lacking in principles and responsibility and their children as marginalized and confused'. In particular, these studies and the negative discussion of their findings 'were particularly vivid in the case of white mothers who had partnered black men, who were generally assumed to be living at the edges of society, isolated and ignorant and with low social and sexual morals' (ibid.). Caballero and Edwards (2010) argue that these attitudes towards mixed families continue to persist nearly a century later, allowing the dominant discourse, which negatively stereotypes mixed families, to persist, to the point where there is a currently popular belief that:

> mothers of mixed racial and ethnic children are likely to be lone parents who have little social contact, with white mothers in particular being abandoned by the children's father, isolated from his family and ostracized by their own.
>
> (ibid., pp. 6–13)

Attitudes have not changed to a great degree

In 2006 *The Guardian* ran an article that discussed the views of Anna Hassan, headteacher of Millfields primary school in Hackney, north-east London (Smith 2006). Anna Hassan's school was described as having 30 per cent of its pupils as being mixed race. In working to support the learning of these children she is quoted as saying:

> Race is supposed to be dead but unfortunately it's alive and kicking in schools, and I think mixed kids are beginning to face the next wave of racism . . . Up until now, mixed-race children have been neglected by people who weren't aware of that.
>
> (ibid.)

Youth workers working in the same area agree with these points, saying that mixed children and young people can have problems finding friendship groups; especially teenagers, whose need to belong is acutely felt. 'When they get to secondary school and children begin to sign up to certain groups, mixed children can find it difficult to fit in' . . . 'Sometimes they are not accepted by black or white groups and they might be cussed about their skin colour or hair' (ibid.).

In particular they point out that, whereas other children 'access their heritage through family connections', for mixed race children 'there can be problems where those are severed' (ibid.). For example:

> Say you are a mixed boy growing up with your white mother who doesn't know about the culture, and your hair's not plaited and your skin's not creamed. You are going to feel self-conscious and will probably be teased at school.
>
> Mixed people can find it difficult to find cultural affiliations . . . They might be rejected by their black side because their skin's too light and their hair's too straight, and rejected by their white side because their skin's too dark and their hair's too frizzy.
>
> (Smith 2006)

Reflective activity

Much work has been done across society in the UK and in EY settings and schools to address racism and to raise teachers' knowledge and understanding about the importance of identity and culture in terms of children's achievement in their learning. However, in this respect education has tended to focus on the culture and identity of children from distinct cultural groups. Mixed race children, however, have families from a range of cultural backgrounds and, therefore, it can be more challenging for schools to know how best to provide support.

Consider the following comments and think about your own practice with regard to mixed race children you work with now, or may work with in the future. If you are mixed race, consider how true you feel these comments to be and what you feel would benefit your colleagues in terms of helping them to better understand the issues.

Obama achieved the dream of becoming the first black president of the USA in January 2009 and his experience of being mixed race – the searching look, the uncertainty of people he meets not knowing who he really is, and their private thoughts of how they may really perceive him – forms part of the general experiences of many mixed race persons. It is an identity that is sometimes characterized as marginal, detached, and confused, an identity that often assumes that individuals wander the world in search of acceptance and belonging.

(Singh and Sumita 2010, p. 99)

Mixed race kids have to expect abuse from both white and black communities – only mixed race couples can understand their experience.

(Thoburn *et al.* 2005, p. 40)

As the figures cited above show, there is *some* link, in some areas, between some mixed race 'populations' and social deprivation. However, research also shows that 'Many teachers assumed/believed that some White/Black Caribbean learners faced "identity problems" linked to fragmented home environments and because they were of mixed heritage' (Mai Sims 2007, p. 14). It is important to also note here the combination of *different* assumptions being made, both about the pupils' home situations *and* about their supposed 'confusion'.

Again, this is part of a wider set of assumptions about children's ethnic backgrounds and their attainment, but with specific assumptions about children of mixed ethnic origins. As discussed by Barn and Harman (2012):

In the academic and popular discourse, there is now a concern that 'mixed families' have become problematized. White mothers in these settings are often subjected to a racialized critical social gaze in a way that their parenting is placed under scrutiny

Barn and Harman (2012) also suggests that, although many cite the 'growing number of mixed relationships' as an indication of how society is becoming more tolerant, 'White mothers of mixed-parentage children can find themselves dealing with racism directed at their children as well as facing social disapproval themselves' (ibid.).

Expectations and assumptions about how mixed race children feel

As the number of children who regard themselves as being mixed race is rising in the UK, and is predicted to reach '1.24m by 2020' (Grimston 2007), unless there is greater awareness about the challenges faced by some children in terms of determining their cultural and ethnic identities there may occur issues of what has become known as 'identity stripping where children and those around them are confused' about 'which community they belong to' (ibid.).

Reflective activity

In our previous discussions about identity and culture we explored how defining aspects of some distinct cultures can be linked to groups of people from specific geographical locations. We have also discussed how children are more likely to achieve in their learning if they see their family's culture being recognised and celebrated in the learning environment. However, for mixed race children their cultural heritage will come from a number of sources. In the same way, although EY settings and schools may feel that they are connecting well with the range of cultural backgrounds their children and families come from, mixed race children do not form a homogeneous group in the same way that children with a Polish background might. Being of mixed race:

> [by] its very nature it is diverse, cutting across cultures, religions, regions, nationalities, histories and ethnicities. There is no such thing as a mix-d community in the geographical sense. The ties of culture, tradition, history and religion do not bind the mix-d population as a separate ethnic grouping. Quite the contrary – many of these things primarily bind mix-d people to other ethnic groups.
> (www.mix-d.org/about/our-contribution-to-the-discussion)

Given what we have just explored in the reflective activity above, there can be a convention that, because those working with mixed race children may be confused about how to approach identity and cultural concerns with them, the children too feel confused about their place in the world. However, this notion has been questioned, and to an extent explored, by recent research. It is certainly the case that many children do feel the need, at some point, to work out their identity, who and where they are, and where they 'fit' into the world; but then, as we have seen in the previous chapter, this may be true of all children. However:

> There is no automatic correspondence between a claimed identity and specific behaviours/attitudes/everyday interactions. Also, one's status as 'mixed' may be central to one person's sense of self, while it may seem to be an afterthought for another individual. What it means to be 'mixed' must be understood in relation to the many other aspects of a person's being: gender, religion, class, hobbies, etc.
>
> (Mai Sims 2007, p. 6)

This is a view supported by others including Singh and Sumita (2010). Singh and Sumita (2010) state that the European and North American view of the importance of an individual identity is, in part, predicated on a particular set of cultural values which forces those whose background does not fit neatly into a binary distinction between this culture or that culture, black or white, to make a choice. Dominant European and North American views on identity and ethnicity want people who are either/or, and generally that means either 'white' or something else. 'It is within these constructions that people of mixed race are perceived as being "between two cultures", or "neither one thing nor another", thus creating an either/or identity' (ibid., p. 100).

Some children, from the beginning, define themselves as 'mixed' and there is a growing community of mixed race people in the UK, brought together on sites such as Intermix (www.intermix.org.uk) and People in Harmony (pih. org.uk). There are smaller projects aimed specifically at children and young people, such as Mix-D (www.mix-d.org) and the Inheritance Project (www. inheritanceproject.org.uk). There is also a move for some young people to locate themselves outside the entire discussion of race.

Case study

Noah's father is white British, and his mother defines herself as British Asian; her parents emigrated to the UK before she was born. The family lives in a multi-racial part of Manchester, and Noah goes to school with children of all kinds of racial origins.

Noah is quite dark-skinned, and is clearly not simply of white British origins. However, the family actively discourages any discussion of race, colour or culture. When anyone asks where his mother is from she says 'North London', and they do not have any particularly Indian things around the house or eat Indian food. It's simply not an issue for him, and he is being brought up to discount it as an issue.

Importantly, even if some children *do* feel confused and 'marooned', it is the role of everyone involved in those children's lives to enable them to find a way through this confusion and establish an identity that they are comfortable with. That may be, as in Noah's case, by ignoring the whole issue of race and identity completely (or at least till a point where he wants to talk about it). For other children, it is important to let them acknowledge all the different parts of their identity, including white parents and family.

Disentangling the conflation of 'mixed race' with 'black/Asian'

Much of the discussion of mixed race children conflates 'mixed race' into black or Asian. This can be useful, especially for children who find themselves the object of racism, as there is wider understanding about *the need to* and *how to* address issues of racism when it is directed at particular ethnicities. However, the current racism debate does not fully address the fact that many children will have two, or more, ethnic origins, cultures and sometimes languages in their family backgrounds. Some children who look black or Asian have white parents and white families, and may spend much or all of their time with those family members. In addition, many children of mixed ethnic origin have neither black nor Asian parents; as some of the examples above demonstrate, they may have parents from Eastern Europe, Latin America, China or other countries. For these reasons, if they have not recently done so, EY settings and schools need to review both their policy on racism and their policy on developing home–school links. Early years settings and schools need to understand the complexities of racism beyond the notion of dealing with overt black/white racist incidents and to understand how racism is also about how children and families can be marginalised in perhaps unwitting ways. Early years settings and schools need to consider how they work with the children and families of mixed race children and what specific aspects of their provision they may need to consider in relation to mixed race children. 'We can no longer think of black and white people as binary opposites'; we need to consider working with children and families in ways that allow 'descriptions of the complexity of cultural and racial mixes' (Singh and Sumita 2010, p. 100).

Reflective activity

Malcolm is a mixed race child in your class. He is doing reasonably well at school and seems to enjoy it, although he is not achieving as well as he could and sometimes he gets upset and starts behaving 'badly'. He also tends to copy a couple of friends of his who start throwing things around the room and refusing to cooperate. You have also been told by a teaching assistant that they heard Malcolm making a racist comment to another child, to which the other child replied 'but you're black too'.

Malcolm's mother is white. She is the person who picks up Malcolm from school and comes to parents' evenings. A parents' evening is due, and you know it is important to talk to her about Malcolm's progress and his behaviour. However, you are unsure about how to tackle the issue about the comments he has been heard making.

Advice from the Pre-school Learning Alliance web-site (www.pre-school.org.uk) states that:

> practitioners may feel a pressure to recognize one heritage above others (in the case of a black/white heritage child, possibly the black rather than the white part of the child's heritage). However, we would recommend acknowledging both or all parts of a child's mixed heritage identity.

In cases such as this, it may be that the child is 'testing out' different aspects of his or her mixed-race heritage and needs both the school and their parents to discuss the situation and help them 'to acknowledge all parts of who' they are (ibid.).

Reflective activity

Below is a list of good practice in terms of supporting mixed race children. Thinking about EY settings and schools you are familiar with, what examples of good practice have you seen?

- The educational setting has books and pictures of children with parents who are visibly ethnically different.
- The educational practitioners make it clear when talking about mixed races figure, such as Mary Seacole, that they had one white and one black parent.
- In discussions about the different festivals families celebrate, it is explored how some families may celebrate festivals from a range of cultural traditions, for example Christmas and Divali.

Beyond the stereotypes: the way real mixed race families live

In reality, most mixed race families do not think about race a lot of the time; they are busy getting on with the daily business of living and bringing up their children. However, there are certainly times at which they negotiate the fact that the parents have different origins and/or ethnicities.

Mixed race families, by definition, bring difference together. Physically, parents look different, and probably children in turn look different from their parents. They may have grown up speaking different languages. One parent may have grown up in a culture in which some of the things that children in the UK take for granted, materially or culturally, were unheard of. Many have negotiated with families of their own which did not want them to 'marry out'. They may, in any case, be thousands of miles away from those families. Or they may both have been brought up in the UK, with apparently very little difference between them apart from skin colour and some issues of family culture – yet still find that there is difference to negotiate.

Families have to work out their own ways of dealing with these complexities. Caballero and colleagues (2008) have looked in some detail at the way parents bring up mixed race children and have identified three main approaches. The first of these approaches (as can be seen illustrated in the first case study below) is what they call:

> the 'individual' one, which doesn't necessarily root a child back into the parents' backgrounds, where parents consider that the children are living their own, 'cosmopolitan' lives, making their own choices about their identity. The actual composition of their child's ethnicity is, quite explicitly, not an issue.
>
> (Cabellero *et al.* 2008, p. 22)

Case study

Jacqueline is 3 years old. Her mother is black British – her family originally came from the Caribbean – and her father is French. Her parents believe that she is 'the face of tomorrow': that she'll have all the possibilities open to her about where and how she wants to live when she grows up. They are very clear that this is not limited (as they would see it) to the UK, the Caribbean or France; they consider her more 'international' than 'mixed race'. Her parents' priority is that she should 'find her own way', but not that this way should be determined by any specifics of Jacqueline's own origins.

Case study

Priya is 4 years old. Her father is from China, and her mother is half English, half German. They are very consciously bringing her up to experience 'both worlds'. They regularly take holidays in Germany and visit China when they can, and her father has taught her basic Mandarin so that she can communicate with her cousins and grandparents. They have also gone to some pains to find pictures and books about 'mixed' families because they live in a fairly mono-racial town, and they want Priya to know that lots of other children come from families similar to her own.

This approach Caballero and colleagues (2008) described as the 'mix' approach, which does root the child's identity back into both backgrounds: the child learns about his or her different heritages and/or the family acknowledges mixing as specific in itself.

Case study

Ahmed's father is Turkish, and his mother is white British. His mother's family were very opposed to her marrying Ahmed's father, and she has cut a lot of her ties to become part of the Turkish community. Ahmed looks very Turkish, and is being brought up to identify as Turkish. He speaks principally Turkish at home, although his mother does talk to him in English and he attends a mainstream English speaking school. He very rarely sees any of his English family.

This approach is described by Caballero and colleagues (2008) as the 'single' approach, whereby one set of origins is prioritised over another.

'Invisible' mixed race children

In our discussions of race and racism we have already briefly explored the notion of colour and how in Europe, and North America to a greater extent, race is about colour and 'racism is a means by which society allocates privilege and status' (Delgado and Stefancic 2001, p. 40). This again returns us to the issue of seeing race as being about the essentialist binary paradigm of black or white (Delgado and Stefancic 2001; Singh and Sumita 2010; Knowles and Lander 2011). However, 'like other paradigms, the black–white one allows people to simplify and make sense of a complex reality' (Delgado and Stefancic 2001). Not only does the black–white paradigm perpetuate the notion that one has to be one or the other but where it is believed it is better to be one rather than the other then it becomes more significant which side the mixed race child decides to identify with. It is certainly explored within Critical Race Theory that being white affords many privileges and a status not so easily afforded to those who are black (Delgado and Stefancic 2001; Niro 2003; Lee 2005; Rodriguez 2005; Knowles and Lander 2011). This notion can often translate into attitudes towards mixed race children that run along the lines of the desire to identify 'all individuals of mixed-race as black' (Sexton 2008, p. 64), which Sexton goes on to say 'is nothing more than a lustful embrace of the mythical concept of white racial purity, and proponents of such an ideology' (ibid.). Alternatively, the children are regarded as being 'lucky enough' to pass as white, so 'what is all the fuss about?'

Some mixed race children do not look 'mixed'. They look either completely like their dark-skinned parent or completely white. For children who look completely black or Asian, their appearance can mean that teachers and other practitioners, for reasons discussed above, do not acknowledge their white family, and all that comes with that (even if they are being brought up in the 'single' approach to identify culturally entirely with their white family). Something as simple as a white parent appearing to pick up a very dark-skinned child may constitute an ordeal, if that parent has to negotiate it again and again at the classroom door.

Children who look white, but have a black or Asian parent, find themselves in a different position, which carries considerable difficulty of its own. On the surface, it may seem that they have avoided all the tensions and issues that 'visibly mixed race' children face; and certainly they are not subjected to the casual racism of passers-by. On the other hand, because they 'pass' so effectively, schools simply assume their whiteness and ignore their other origins (especially in areas where most or all children are still from white UK backgrounds).

As a last thought about mixed race children and their families, which, if you are mixed race, you may identify with, for those people who work with children and families it is important to realise that racial diversity in families is not always obvious and that a family's racial and cultural make-up cannot be assumed simply on the basis of physical appearance. What is important is that we consider how EY settings and schools reflect the cultures of the children and families they work with and through that reflection enable children to achieve in their learning.

Case study

Priya is in reception. Her mother is from India, and her father is white British. Priya looks completely white, with red hair and fair skin.

In terms of her upbringing, Priya's family take a 'mix' verging on a 'single' approach. Because of her parents' work with an international agency, she has lived in India and a lot of the 'culture' of her home is

4 Immigrant, refugee and asylum seeker families

Gianna Knowles

This chapter explores:

- how being a refugee or asylum seeker is different from being an immigrant;
- a recent history of migration to Britain and across Europe;
- migrants arriving in the UK from Eastern Europe;
- who migrates to the UK and why;
- why families seek refuge or asylum;
- children seeking asylum and refugee status;
- how best to support asylum seeker children in their learning; and
- Britain's ethnically diverse society.

In 2010 the government's department of national statistics published a report entitled 'Ethnicity: Introductory User Guide'. The report states that 'ethnicity describes ancestry, heritage, religion, culture, nationality, language and religion' (Office for National Statistics and ESDS Government 2010, p. 5). *The Guardian* newspaper, reporting statistics from the same department, states that in 2009 the non-white British population was recorded as being 9.1 million, out of a total population of 54 million (i.e. 16.8 per cent) (Rogers 2011). They also show that of the 432 local authorities within the UK, in 225 up to 96.5 per cent of the population is white, while in some areas of the country there is much greater diversity of ethnicities: in the London Borough of Brent, for example, 'just over a third of its population counts as white British, with large mixed race, Asian, Black and Irish' (ibid.). These figures tell us that the vast majority of the population in the UK is white British and that the ethnic minorities found in the UK can be people from, or with a heritage of, many different countries including, more recently, Eastern Europe.

How being a refugee or asylum seeker is different from being an immigrant

There can sometimes be confusion about what it means for children and families to have migrated to the UK and are immigrants, compared with those who have come to the UK seeking asylum, or who have been granted refugee status and leave to remain in the UK. Briefly, it is usually the case that those who migrate to the UK have applied to do so and arrive with the necessary paperwork and visas already issued by the Home Office and UK's border agency. Immigration requires a visa and will have been a planned move from one country to another, with all that planning a move of this nature entails. Those who arrive in the UK who are seeking asylum are doing so because they have been driven from their own country by factors that make it unsafe to remain there. For children and families, a planned move will be very different from flight from a dangerous situation. Indeed, in such situations, some members of the family may have been left behind or their whereabouts may be unknown. The section below explores these distinctions in more detail.

Migration: a recent history of migration to Britain and across Europe

> The post-Second World War era heralded a new phase in the history of immigration. Migration increased significantly in volume and included mass movements of European refugees to Western Europe, the large-scale migration of qualified personnel from Europe to North America and Australia, and the migration from former colonies to Britain, France and the Netherlands.
>
> (Herbert 2008, p. 14)

The movement of peoples across continents and across Europe since 1945 has been occasioned by a number of factors. The end of the Second World War saw a global dislocation of peoples, in both physical and financial terms. Countries lay in ruins as a result of war damage and on the brink of bankruptcy as a result of paying for war armaments. Perhaps more so than at any other time in history, the peoples of many countries were united in their need to work, in this instance to rebuild their lives from the destruction of the second global war in the space of 50 years. The two world wars of the first part of the twentieth century not only brought with them death and destruction in a physical sense, but in the UK also heralded the end of 'old' notions of rigid class hierarchies and social stratifications, and were the final blow to the already failing European empires in Africa and Asia.

As a result of the final disbanding of the British Empire and the need for cheap labour to rebuild Britain after the Second World War, migration of people from Asia, particularly India, Pakistan and Bangladesh, reached 9 million by the end of the twentieth century, Britain being 'their single most important destination' (Herbert 2008, p. 14). In its post-war rebuilding, 'Britain turned to its former colonial territories, including the Caribbean and the Indian subcontinent, for a cheap workforce' (ibid.). As a result of the British Nationality Act 1948, nationals of what later became 'former' British colonies became UK citizens with British passports and, therefore, had the same rights to live in the UK as those born in the UK. As Herbert (ibid.)

states, just as Britain had once colonised these countries as 'a source of cheap raw materials, the colonies were now a source of cheap labour'. However, because of the perceived unpopularity of this policy with some sectors of the UK white population 'The Commonwealth Immigration Act 1962 introduced a voucher system designed to curb "coloured" migration' (Herbert 2008, p. 16).

The BBC History web-site (www.bbc.co.uk/history/) carries many stories of people from the former British colonies in the Caribbean who migrated to the UK after 1945. Many Caribbean men had fought as members of British armed forces in the war and after the war thought they would be coming to a welcoming 'mother country' where they could find good jobs and decent housing for themselves and their families. However, as the brief extracts from stories below show, the reality of migrating to Britain rarely lived up to expectations:

> They tell you it is the 'mother country', you're all welcome, you all British. When you come here you realise you're a foreigner and that's all there is to it.
>
> The average person knows you as a colonial and that's all. You cut cane or carry bananas and that's it. Anybody wants to diddle you they say I just come off the banana boat and things like that.
>
> (BBC 2012a)

People of the Commonwealth and the armed forces 1939–40

By the end of the Second World War in 1945 over 3 million men from the British Empire and Dominions had been enlisted for service in Britain's armed forces:

> 1,440,500 from India, 629,000 from Canada, 413,000 from Australia, 136,000 from South Africa, 128,500 from New Zealand and more than 134,000 from other colonies.
>
> Of the thousands of men from the Caribbean who joined the British army many were sent to Europe for training . . . Approximately 5,500 West Indian RAF personnel came to Britain in 1944–5. From 1944, West Indian women served in the Women's Auxiliary Air Force (WAAF) and the Auxiliary Territorial Service (ATS) in Britain. Over 40,000 workers volunteered to live and work as agricultural labourers in the USA.
>
> (BBC 2012b)

However, such was the reality of migrating to the UK that by the mid-1960s significant numbers of Caribbean migrants returned to their countries of origin (Plaza and Henry 2006). As Plaza and Henry (2006, p. 1) comment:

> many of the returnees have had difficult lives abroad working, often for only minimum wage, at jobs that were menial and hazardous to their long-term health. Most kept their hardships and lifestyles in the metropolitan countries a secret from family and kin in the Caribbean, because they feared losing admiration for their decision to migrate.

During the time of the British Empire in Africa, many from Britain's Asian colonies had been encouraged by the British to migrate for work to British colonies in Africa. By 1968, when most African colonies were independent of Britain and other European colonisers, some African countries began an Africanisation programme (Herbert 2008). The governments of Kenya, Uganda, Tanzania and Malawi 'sought to eradicate the economic dominance of South Asians that had developed under British rule' (ibid., p. 15). As a result of this programme, by 1972 Uganda's government led by General Idi Amin had expelled approximately 55,000 South Asians from Uganda; over half of these peoples held British passports and arrived in the UK (ibid.).

The most recent migrants to call attention to themselves are those arriving in the UK from Eastern Europe

UK tabloid newspaper headlines

British bosses snub UK jobless for Romanians
(www.thesun.co.uk, 4 February 2012)

TAXPAYERS are supporting more than a quarter of a million immigrants who have come to Britain from outside the EU
(www.thesun.co.uk, 20 January 2012)

Secret report warns of migration meltdown in Britain. Our investigation found Poles are dumping children in local care homes so they can travel to Britain. Some reportedly killed themselves after being left behind . . . East European immigrants living rough are becoming drunk and aggressive, and flooding homeless hostels.
(Walters 2012)

Such newspaper headlines mask the reality of the situation with regard to migration. For example: 'the white British population has stayed the same since 2001 – because even though there has been an increase in births, there has also been a similar number of people migrating' (Rogers 2011). There is also the notion that, although people may, in the short or medium term, move from their own countries believing there to be better economic opportunities abroad, 'migrants are often pulled back to their countries of birth because this is often the location where they feel a cultural affiliation and a level of comfort' (Plaza and Henry 2006, p. 4). In 2009 the web-site Immigration Matters (www.immigrationmatters.co.uk) reported that 66,000 Eastern European migrants returned to their own countries that year, leaving behind concern that:

> As Eastern European workers return home in droves, how will the care sector recruit sufficient numbers of staff to fill their vacancies for care workers, which are already on the Government's official Shortage Occupations list?
>
> (www.immigrationmatters.co.uk)

Indeed, this last point also raises another issue often ignored by those wishing to negatively sensationalise aspects of migration: those who work in the UK contribute to the UK economy both through their taxes and through spending their wages and salaries. European Economic Area (EEA) rules applying to migration are also open to use by UK nationals who wish to migrate within the EEA.

Spain attracts record levels of immigrants seeking jobs and sun

> Some 47,000 Britons, equivalent to the entire population of a town the size of Kettering or Hereford, signed on as new residents at Spanish town halls last year. That brought the registered British population in Spain to 274,000 – equivalent to a city the size of Bradford or Leicester . . . But experts estimate that up to three times as many Britons, about 750,000 people, spend a significant part of the year living in Spain.
>
> (Tremlett 2006)

It is perhaps not surprising that many UK nationals who migrate to other countries in the EEA do so for the same reasons people migrate to the UK; they believe job opportunities are going to be better for them. The reality of those from the UK migrating to other countries can, however, be as it is for non-nationals coming to the UK. On arriving at their destination many UK nationals find that they are offered only low-paid unskilled work, the availability of which fluctuates depending on the economic situation in the country. Most countries have their own regulations governing the qualifications needed for particular employment in that country and often migrants will arrive to find they do not have the documents that will enable them to gain the employment they hoped for.

The current economic crisis in Europe has also caused the press and governments across Europe to focus on managing the perceived challenges caused by the number of EEA migrants, including UK nationals, who have been moving around the EEA during the past 10 years. As the BBC reports (Rainsford 2011): '32% of Spain's immigrant workers are unemployed, compared with 21.3% of the overall workforce. Many are now losing their residency rights and facing expulsion . . . There is a rise of xenophobia and racism'. UK nationals migrating within the EEA have also found that unfavourable exchange rates between sterling and other currencies, particularly the euro, have meant that savings and pensions they have taken with them have left them financially worse off, not better, outside the UK. Similarly, whereas all health care is free in the UK through the National Health Service, this is not necessarily so across the EEA. This is what Plaza and Henry (2006) refer to as the 'disappointment theory', explaining why migrants return to their country of origin and why, as with many migrants of all nationalities, many UK migrants have returned to the UK.

Reading the headlines of tabloid newspapers tells only part of the story about migration and the actual picture of who is immigrating to the UK and why.

How many people migrate to the UK?

The big number in today's story is the net migration of 250,000 people – the difference between the 593,000 people who came into the country in the year to June 2011 and the 343,000 who left the country to live abroad for more than 12 months.

(Rogers 2012)

The statistics show that those who migrated to the UK in 2011 came from the following countries:

- 11.9 per cent from India;
- 5.8 per cent from Pakistan;
- 5.4 per cent from Poland;
- 5.2 per cent from Australia; and

- 5.2 per cent from China.

Most people emigrating from the UK go to Australia, followed by the USA (ibid.).

The regulations on migration to the UK and across the EEA and Switzerland are set out below.

European Economic Area migration to Britain

- **Visitors** to the UK are allowed to stay for up to 6 months.
- Most people wishing to stay in the UK for **longer than 6 months** need to **apply for a visa to remain** in the UK and to check their status with regard to non-visitor immigration categories.
- For those immigrants from within the **EEA or Switzerland** who wish to remain in the UK for 6 months or longer, and possibly work in the UK, the following rules apply:
  - Those deemed **high-value** migrants – investors, entrepreneurs, exceptionally talented people and recent graduates from UK universities – can apply to enter or stay in the UK without needing a job offer. However, they will need to pass a points-based assessment.
  - **Skilled workers** who have been offered a job in the UK and have a sponsor can apply to come to the UK and remain.
  - Some **temporary workers** may be allowed to work in the UK for a short period.

(Home Office UK Border Agency 2012)

Migration to Britain for people from outside the European Economic Area or Switzerland

- **Visitors** to the UK are allowed to stay for up to 6 months.
- Most people wishing to stay in the UK for **longer than 6 months** need to **apply for a visa to remain** in the UK and to check their status with regard to non-visitor immigration categories.

Someone from outside the EEA or Switzerland who wishes to migrate to the UK and remain in the UK for longer than 6 months needs, in the first instance, to apply for a visa to enter the UK. Being granted a visa to reside in the UK, to work or to settle is very complex and will depend on the country the migrant is applying from, or is a national of.

For the most detailed information about how to migrate to the UK, or to find out more about who is entitled to migrate to the UK check the Home Office UK Border Agency's web-site: www.ukba.homeoffice.gov. uk/.

Those most likely to be granted visas are:

- people who are family members of those who are British citizens and/or settled persons. These may be partners, children or elderly relatives;
- those coming to study and possibly their family members;
- family members of migrant workers;
- family members of those granted asylum; and
- those who wish to get married or register a civil partnership in the UK, whether they intend visiting or staying in the UK.

(Home Office UK Border Agency 2012)

Seeking asylum in the UK

In stark contrast to those who migrate to the UK, those seeking asylum who come to Britain are leaving their own countries for very different reasons. 'Asylum seekers are people who flee their home country and seek refugee status in another country, possibly because of war or human rights abuses' (DfE 2012a).

How many people seek asylum in the UK?

- In 2009, the courts overturned Home Office decisions in 28 per cent of asylum appeals (British Refugee Council 2012).
- In 2010, 17,916 applications for asylum were made in the UK (Rogers 2012).
- In 2011, 60,244 people were removed from the UK (ibid.).

Under the United Nations Convention of Human Rights, to which the UK is a signatory, it is recognised that individuals and families are sometimes unsafe in the countries they live in and therefore need to seek a place of safety in another country. Article 14 of the United Nations Convention of Human

Rights states: 'everyone has the right to seek and to enjoy in other countries asylum from persecution' (www.un.org). The UK, along with at least 47 other countries, has signed an agreement to uphold the rights outlined in the convention. However, as a convention or declaration, the document is not 'binding on member states in international law' (Foster 2008, p. 17); signing merely indicates that the UK is committed to upholding these rights. In this way, the UK, both through being a signatory to such conventions and through aspects of its own law, recognises that some individuals and families will need, for many reasons, to flee their own countries, or the countries they are living in, to seek asylum in a country that will better protect their safety.

However, fleeing to a safer country does not automatically mean the individual or family will be granted asylum in the country they flee to. In the UK, for example, on arrival the asylum seeker must declare that they are seeking asylum and 'lodge an application for asylum with the [UK Government]' (DfE 2012a). If the application is successful the applicant will be granted refugee status and will be given limited leave to remain in the UK. If, after 5 years, the person or persons are still in the UK their status will be reviewed to determine if they still qualify for refugee status and need to continue to be granted asylum. Those granted refugee status before 2005 have indefinite leave to remain (ILR) and do not need to have their case reviewed after 5 years (www.refugeecouncil.org.uk/practice/basics/process). Those who are not granted refugee status and asylum in Britain must leave the UK. Some refused asylum seekers will voluntarily return to their country; others are forcibly returned.

Under the 1951 United Nations Convention Relating to the Status of Refugees a refugee is defined as:

> A person who owing to a well-founded fear of being persecuted for reasons of race, religion, nationality, membership of a particular social group or political opinion, is outside the country of his nationality and is unable or, owing to such fear, is unwilling to avail himself of the protection of that country; or who, not having a nationality and being outside the country of his former habitual residence as a result of such events, is unable or, owing to such fear, is unwilling to return to it.
>
> (UNHCR 2011, p. 14)

Those seeking asylum do not fall into an easy category to define, which is why applications for asylum and to be a refugee in the UK are dealt with on a case by case basis. However, at the back of most Europeans' minds when they think about the need to give asylum are memories, actual or historical, of the failure of many countries to help Jewish people fleeing Germany and trying to seek asylum in the 1930s and early 1940s. As Rosenthal and Barry (2009, p. 238) write:

> The tragic and shameful failure of many countries, including Canada and the United States, to accept Jews seeking asylum in the late 1930s and

even the 1940s remains a vivid memory today and provides much of the moral impetus for the maintenance of a refugee regime that includes the right to asylum as one of its components.

Neither can Britain's record of help for Jewish people seeking refugee status at the time bear much scrutiny. Throughout the 1930s Britain and the United States of America severely limited the number of Jewish immigrants to their respective countries (Caron 1998; Kestenberg and Kahn 1998; Rosenthal and Barry 2009). Britain attended the Evian Conference in 1938, the outcome of which further limited Britain's acceptance of Jewish asylum seekers fleeing Nazi Germany (Beller 2007). In the late 1930s as part of the *Kindertransport* operation Britain did receive some of the 10,000 children who fled Germany. However, many of the parents of these children were not granted visas to enter the UK and stories of 'the trauma of sudden separation from their parents and the consequent shock of abandonment' suffered and overcome by many of these children can be found on many web-sites documenting the Holocaust (Kestenberg and Kahn 1998, p. 105).

Reflective activity

Following the huge international devastation of the Second World War, which, in the space of 5 years, left many countries, particularly Europe, in ruins, many of the countries that experienced the terrible destruction, loss of life and dislocation of its people came together for the United Nations Conference on International Organization and signed The Charter of the United Nations on 26 June 1945. The mandate of the United Nations today is:

- to save succeeding generations from the scourge of war, which twice in our lifetime has brought untold sorrow to mankind, and
- to reaffirm faith in fundamental human rights, in the dignity and worth of the human person, in the equal rights of men and women and of nations large and small, and
- to establish conditions under which justice and respect for the obligations arising from treaties and other sources of international law can be maintained, and
- to promote social progress and better standards of life in larger freedom.

(Charter of the United Nations 2012)

Consider the wars and acts of genocide that have occurred since 1945 and reflect on how successful the UN has been in living up to these intentions. For example, Britain has been involved in conflicts in Northern Ireland, India, Palestine, Malaya, Korea, the Suez Canal Zone, Kenya, Oman, Dhofar, the Falklands, Bosnia, Kosovo, Sierra Leone, Iraq and elsewhere.

As we can see from the reflective activity above, war, conflict and the oppression of people by their own governing regimes is still a significant issue in many countries. All war and oppression will generate refugees. The decision taken by families and individuals to leave their home is one that may be a necessary immediate response to a threatening situation that has seemingly suddenly developed. Many families that become refugees do not have passports or the resources to buy tickets to travel by train, air or bus to other countries; many are in a position where they can only try to walk to safety. For these reasons many of those who become refugees do so in countries that neighbour their own. Since Britain is an island it is not necessarily easy to travel to and it is in part for the reasons just discussed that 'the UK is home to less than 2% of the world's refugees – out of 16 million' children and adults worldwide who are refugees (UNHCR 2008). Further UN figures show, for example, that:

- Over 520,000 refugees have fled the conflict in Sudan to neighbouring countries, 'yet only 265 Sudanese people applied for asylum in the UK in 2008' (ibid.).
- About 80 per cent of the world's refugees are living in developing countries, often in camps. Africa and Asia between them host more than three-quarters of the world's refugees. 'Europe looks after 14%' (ibid.).

The Refugee Council (n.d.) in the UK also states that:

> The likelihood that a refugee will be recognised as having protection needs and granted status depends on the country where they apply for asylum. In Europe, the proportion of people granted asylum varies widely, from 3% in Slovenia to 77% in Finland (2008 figures for initial decisions from UNHCR, June 2009).

Having arrived in the UK to seek asylum and refugee status, the asylum seeker is not allowed to work in the UK. On arrival in the UK, those seeking asylum are taken from the UK immigration check points to removal centres, previously known as detention centres. Removal centres are holding centres for foreign nationals awaiting decisions on their asylum claims or awaiting deportation following a failed application (politics.co.uk 2012). The Home Office's UK Border Agency says of its removal centres that:

We provide a high standard of facilities in our centres. These include libraries, formal education classes and access to on-the-job training. We aim to help detainees make the best use of their time and to prepare them for their return home.

(UK Border Agency 2012)

The centres also provide health care, including dental care and optical care; they also seek to provide mental health services. Those seeking asylum do not have permission to work in the UK. A small minority of those seeking asylum receive some income support and housing benefit; 'However, the numbers of asylum seekers supported by benefits or by local authorities is very small, and is continually decreasing as decisions are made on their cases' (DfES 2004, p. 3).

Reflective activity

Despite the low numbers of asylum seekers who come to Britain, compared with the global number of those seeking asylum, and the tight controls on those who arrive here seeking refugee status, we have seen above how there are a number of negative stereotypes about those seeking asylum that still appear in the British media. Indeed the UN itself has commented on the often widespread negative view of asylum seekers in the UK.

UNHCR has continued to express its grave concern that the UK's tabloid press continues to publish inaccurate and misleading stories which are a danger to good community relations. UNHCR's concerns that incorrect and alarmist reporting propagates an atmosphere of fear and hostility towards foreigners, including asylum seekers and refugees, remain despite the PCC's guidance.

Media must reflect the diverse needs and situations of asylum seekers and refugees, young and old, male and female.

(Joint Committee on Human Rights 2007)

Case study

Farah is now 19 years old. She talks about how her mother put her and her brother on a plane to the UK in 2003; it was the last time she saw her mother. Both her parents are now dead. She says she was terrified and clung to her mother refusing to leave her, but her mother was strong and made her go. They were supposed to be met by their aunt who was already living in Britain, but she had been delayed as it was difficult to get the message to her that they were arriving. Farah talks of how scared she was when they arrived and did not know what to do and how they spent 2 days in a detention centre until her aunt had managed to sort out what was happening; how there were other Iranians and other Iranian children in the centre and they looked after them.

She says she still gets very sad when she thinks about her parents, but she and her brother were lucky because they had their aunt to come to. She knows of other refugee children who were placed in care, some, particularly from Somalia, who entirely lost contact with their families. She says that she and her brother went though some tough times but now she is in her first year at university studying law with a view to being a human rights lawyer.

Farah's story mirrors that of many refugees who speak of the fear and loneliness of being a refugee, of missing home, family and familiar things, while all the time trying to come to terms with what has happened and deal with the confusion and dislocation caused by being in a new country. They talk of the pain of not knowing what has happened to loved ones left behind, or of not having had the chance to bury or mourn dead family members. They talk of the sometimes seemingly heartless treatment of the UK asylum process, of having to share living space with people from all nationalities and cultures, some of whom are very traumatised. They speak of the humiliation of not being able to support and care for their families. However, there are also stories of great hope and humanity and examples of the care and support they have found from individuals and organisations seeking to provide the best support they can.

For more stories told by refugees visit www.refugeestories.org.

Children seeking asylum and refugee status

Although most asylum-seeking children arrive in the UK with one or both parents, some do not. They may arrive with friends or relatives who are not their usual carers, or they may arrive as unaccompanied asylum-seeking children like Farah and her brother. The United Nations High Commissioner for Refugees defines an unaccompanied asylum-seeking child as being someone under 18 years old and not cared for by the child's usual carers. In the event that there is no suitable adult to care for these children, the responsibility rests with the social services department of the local authority and the children are cared for under the provisions of the Children Act 1989 (DfES 2004, p. 3).

Supporting asylum seeker children in their learning

In this way children who are seeking asylum, or who have refugee status in the UK, will come from very diverse backgrounds. Children who may come under the term 'asylum seeker' or 'refugee' cannot be lumped together as a homogeneous group. The children will have fled their own countries for many different reasons and will have backgrounds that vary from one another in terms of ethnicity, culture and life experiences, particularly in terms of what led to the need to seek asylum.

Reflective activity

In working with children who are seeking asylum or who have refugee status, early years (EY) settings and schools need to ensure they have considered some of the following issues.

• Many children will have suffered or witnessed horrific experiences in their home countries and flight to the UK, and for a small number this may affect their ability to learn and rebuild their lives (DfE 2012a).

• Although these children may have been in education for a number of years, their education may have been interrupted by the situation that lead them to flee their home.

• Many children who come to the UK seeking asylum or who are refugees are not living with one or both of their parents.

• Those looking after the children, if they are also seeking asylum or are refugees, may also have suffered or witness terrible things and may be in a traumatised state so that they are emotionally absent in terms of looking after the child (ibid.).

• The children will often have come from a financially secure home, since, as we have seen, only those who have the funds to do so can reach the UK. However, as an asylum seeker or refugee they may now be living in a low-income household or in poverty.

• Children may speak little or no English on arrival in the UK (ibid.).

Where EY settings and schools have not fully thought through what is needed to support children who are seeking asylum or who are refugees, it is also often the case that the children 'will suffer racist bullying or isolation in school' (ibid.).

Britain's ethnically diverse society

Moving to another country is not often something attempted lightly by anyone. To move country requires not only the necessary paperwork to be in place but some sense of knowing what is waiting at the other end. Perhaps not surprisingly most migrating peoples seek to first settle in areas where there are already people *like themselves*: people who speak their language, eat their food and dress in ways that are familiar to them. In Chapter 2 we have discussed how people often seek to be with like-minded others to reinforce their own identities. For these reasons, where there are significant numbers of people migrating they can be perceived as sticking together in ways that alienate other groups. By the 1960s many of the migrants from former colonies coming to the UK after 1945 began to be regarded by some sectors of society and media as *a problem*. Notoriously some right-wing politicians such as Sir Oswald Mosley fuelled these resentments and the late 1950s saw violence towards black communities in Nottingham and parts of London.

Government policy approaches to understanding and managing the increasing diversity of cultures and religions in the UK and managing the tensions that seemed to be surfacing in the late 1950s and early 1960s have passed through a number of phases. Initially, it was expected by many that migrants to the UK would be assimilated into existing dominant British culture. However, the concern with this notion is that it privileges 'the interests and lifestyles of the descendants of the dominant group' (Coello 2010, p. 22), which goes against long-standing traditions of liberty and freedom of expression central to both UK law and tradition. Therefore, in terms of responding to the increasingly ethnically diverse population of the UK, one of the first policy responses was to adopt a *multicultural* approach. Multiculturalism is rooted in the notion that everyone has the 'liberty to explore' and choose what, for them, 'is the best concept of what is the "good life"' (ibid., p. 21), choosing to follow whatever cultural and religious practices they see as enabling them to achieve what they want from life.

In this way, all cultural approaches to life can exist side by side without interfering with or damaging each other. Through a range of government policies and through the natural ways demographics of countries change and evolve over time, over the past 50 years the UK has, in the main, sought to move to a situation in which 'institutions and organisations create equal opportunities for all members of society' (ibid., p. 22), the ultimate goal being a society that allows 'peaceful coexistence amongst diverse groups' (ibid.). In trying to achieve this aim one of the tensions that has yet to be fully reconciled is whether those who come to the UK as immigrants or seeking asylum should integrate into the existing culture or actively pursue and keep alive the culture they experienced in their home countries. However, to polarise these issues into these two simple extremes serves only to perpetuate this line of argument, rather than work towards a solution.

Britain, arguably, never was a country with one homogeneous culture. What research does show is that, in order to enable groups of people from diverse ethnicities and cultures to live together in ways that are mutually beneficial, what is needed is that those groups that do dominate, financially and politically, must show that they support 'strong efforts at fighting prejudice and discrimination' (ibid., p. 24) and actively seek to provide real equality of opportunity for all, rather than having a society in which there are winners and losers. Only when this is available to all, regardless of ethnicity, gender or class, will society work towards some form of homogeneity. In relation to this notion Coello (2010, p. 47) comments:

> The commitment of British political elites has been consistent throughout the years in stressing positive relations amongst the different communities in society, resulting in a positive self-reflection of what it means to be British as well as a positive perception of minorities. This is reflected in an increasing participation of public and private organisations in diversity policies.

Early years settings and primary schools have a considerable part to play in this process, since they are spaces where children and families from diverse backgrounds can begin to explore what it might mean to grow up and create a society that can manage a range of alternative identities and cultures, or what Sarat and Kearns (2001, p. 3) refer to as 'the good' society. The good society for them is:

> one in which groups can be valued for their distinct cultures and ways of being. The good society values diversity as the basis of inclusion. Shared citizenship is not based on a universally shared culture or common identity. Cultural pluralism asks us to acknowledge and embrace difference, "rather than assuming . . . that there was a neutral, acultural institutional reality, in public schools or other places".

(ibid., p. 4)

5   Step-families and step-parenting

Gianna Knowles

This chapter explores:

- how one in three people are in a step-family situation;
- what is meant by step-parenting and step-families and the range and complexity of step-families;
- negotiating and understanding relationships with existing and new family members;
- losing old families and the impact of attachment and loss;
- that the dominant discourse about 'nuclear families' can marginalise the experience of those living in step-families;
- the extended family – staying in touch with family members; and
- early years (EY) settings and schools working with step-families.

One in three people are in a step-family situation

In terms of the diversity of family groupings this book explores, the one that most readers will have some insight into is that of the step-family. Many of you will have direct experience of being step-parented, or of being a step-parent yourself. Some of the issues discussed in this book are specific to certain groups in society; however, the step-family crosses all sectors and groups; it is not specific to class or ethnicity and, therefore, is an aspect of family diversity that many will be able to relate to. The term 'step' in this context usually refers to those in a family relationship because of marriage, rather than because there is a biological connection. The most usual model of family to which the term is applied is where one or both of the adults or parents in the family are parenting a child, or children, of whom they are not the birth parent, but because they have married one of the parents of the child, or children. Often the step-parent will have been in a prior marriage or relationship too and have children from that relationship, therefore the children in the family may have step-parents and step-siblings.

Step-families have always existed; however, prior to changes to divorce law in the 1950s and access to legal aid in the late 1940s step-families more usually occurred because of the death of one of the adults in a marriage.

Historically, in many instances step-families were formed because of the death of mothers in childbirth, or through maternal mortality. Although it is hard to find exact statistics for the rates of maternal mortality (death in childbirth, or because of birth-related complications), Loudon (1992) discusses how gradually, although not always in a smooth progression, the rates of maternal mortality have dropped significantly over the past 200 years. In discussing the difficulty of gaining precise data about the exact rates of death in childbirth he is, however, quite clear that the high rates of maternal mortality, compared with recent data, 'were never exaggerated – they under estimated the true level' (Loudon cited in Dever 1998, p. 18). Loudon (1992) claims that particularly in the 1870s the rates of death in childbirth were unusually high and that they did not begin to fall generally, down to their current level, until the mid-nineteenth century.

What is meant by step-parenting and step-families and the range and complexity of having 'step' relations

The creation of step-families through divorce and re-marriage began to become the more usual reason for the creation of step-families, particularly as laws with regard to divorce began to change in the first half of the twentieth century. Smart (1999) notes how the trend in divorce started rising before 1950. In part, this was because of the introduction of legal aid in 1949; without access to financial support to pay for legal costs divorce was just too expensive for many people. This is not to say that marriages did not break down before 1949, simply that the only option where a marriage had failed and those involved had found new partners was for people to co-habit with new partners rather than re-marry. In 1969 the divorce laws changed allowing a marriage to be dissolved 'on the sole ground of "irretrievable breakdown"' (Smart 1999, p. 7), whereas the previous grounds for divorce were those of cruelty, adultery or desertion, which not only were comparatively costly to prove, but also apportioned considerable blame to one party.

More recently the statistics show that over the past 20 years the UK, and much of the rest of Europe, has continued to see a steady increase in the number of marriages that have ended in divorce. Garralda (2010, p. 50), citing the European Foundation for the Improvement of Living and Working Conditions figures for divorce, claims that 'across the 25 countries of the European Union where 9% to 49% of marriages ended in divorce in the 1990s, 2003 saw an increase from 13% to 75%'. With specific regard to the increase of step-families as a response to the rise in divorce rates in the west generally, Arnaut and colleagues (2000, p. 111) state that 'Americans born in the 1980s have a 1 in 2 chance of being in a stepfamily either as children or adults'. They also add as a rider to this comment that 60 per cent of second marriages also end in divorce (ibid.). Where second marriages break down in this way the children involved can then be in a situation of losing not only a step-parent, who they may have formed a very strong relationship with, but also step-brothers and sisters who, again, they will have often regarded as being family, thus adding a further layer of complexity in terms of emotional and legal relationships.

With regard to the legal position vis-á-vis the step-parent–step-child relationship, it is helpful to note that in England and Wales the mother has automatic parental responsibility for children, from their birth. Parental responsibility does not, however, apply in the same way to fathers.

> In England and Wales, if the parents of a child are married to each other at the time of the birth, or if they have jointly adopted a child, then they both have parental responsibility. Parents do not lose parental responsibility if they divorce, and this applies to both the resident and the non-resident parent.
>
> (www.direct.gov.uk/en/Parents/ParentsRights/DG_4002954)

Living with the mother, even for a long time, does not give a father parental responsibility and 'if the parents are not married, parental responsibility does not always pass to the natural father if the mother dies' (ibid.). In terms of a step-parent having parental responsibility for a child, this can happen only through the legal adoption process or if the step-parent applies for parental responsibility through the courts. When a child has both parents still living a step-parent needs the agreement of both the child's parents or, depending on the circumstances surrounding the application for parental responsibility, parental responsibility may be awarded by order of the court (www.direct.gov.uk/en/Parents/Adoptionfosteringandchildrenincare/AdoptionAndFostering/DG_10021340).

Current UK law under the 1989 Children Act does make provision for children to be consulted about who they wish to live with, in the event of divorce. However, in effect, it is often those with parental responsibility for children who are the prime instigators in deciding the custody arrangements for children after a divorce (Brannen *et al*. 2000; Timms *et al*. 2007). Children, however, have very strong views about being consulted about what happens to them after divorce or separation. The research of Brannen and colleagues (2000) and the NSPCC (Timms *et al*. 2007) shows that 'The great majority of children supported the principle of children having a say in decisions concerning where they should reside following the break-up' (Brannen *et al*. 2000, p. 38). However, EY settings and schools are allowed to contact only those who have parental responsibility for children. This can be difficult for all parties, since in the event of divorce and separation parents who do not have parental responsibility for, or custody of, their children may feel that they are being further excluded from the lives of their children. Similarly, children will have strong feelings about who they regard as 'parents', including step-parents, and who they want to talk about, write about and contact with regard to what is happening to them at school and in all aspects of their lives. For these reasons, EY settings and schools need to be mindful of the legal position with regard to parental responsibility, but also sensitive to the feelings of the children in these situations.

Having discussed what can seem like very negative issues surrounding family breakdown and the complexity of step-family relationships, we must also remind ourselves that 'despite the findings on the long-lasting and pervasive consequences of divorce, the majority of children who experience parental divorce do not go on to show disturbance over time' (Garralda 2010, p. 51).

Negotiating the relationships in step-families

As we have seen, there are a large number of adults and children who live in a step-family network, networks which often extend across more than one household. Many of those 'entering' a step-family relationship come to it with already formed attitudes and values about what they expect a family to be like, and building working relationships as a new step-family can take years (Robinson 1993). There can be a temptation to think of this as being more difficult for a step-family than for a traditionally constituted nuclear family; however, even the briefest reflection on all family life shows that it is often a place where rules, needs, wants and expectations of various family members are constantly being formed and renegotiated. What is different for step-families and can be challenging, in terms of negotiating family rules and relationships, is managing the mobility, both physically and emotionally, of children between the parents and households they have connections with. Again, how adults and children view these arrangements may vary enormously. For most parents involved in any family situation one of their primary concerns is the day-to-day care and welfare of the children in the family. Adults also need to take into consideration pragmatic issues to do with time and money. For example, arranging the physical complexities of a child's, or children's, mobility between a number of households takes organisation. It also presupposes that all the adults involved in the situation are in agreement with arrangements and are prepared to discuss the finer details with each other. Where an adult may make a decision based on what is pragmatically the best thing to do, a child can see this as adult control and coercion, rather than care (Brannen *et al.* 2000). These tensions can add to the challenge of making a new step-family 'work'.

Case study

Aisha says:

> when Ali and I first got together trying to sort out family weekends was really difficult. I would make arrangements for my son to see his dad and Ali would arrange for his two to come here. My ex-husband would sometimes say 'well I can't do that date', or he couldn't pick

Rafiq up, or some other problem. Then I was upset for Rafiq, but had to stay calm and fit in with what my ex wanted and then Ali would say 'why do we always do what he wants'. Then Rafiq would find out we had arranged to take Ali's two to the cinema and he'd want to come too and not see his dad.

It is also worth noting that parents trying to negotiate their way through the first few months of a new step-family can feel an added pressure in that they are concerned about how the family is appearing to those on the outside of the family, to EY settings and schools for example, since parents are expected to care for and regulate not only day-to-day life inside the family, but also how family members appear and behave in the wider world. In this respect, parents may appear defensive or aggressive and require support and understanding from others for what they are trying to manage, rather than perceived criticism of their management of a difficult and stressful time.

How children manage and understand the relationships they have with step-family members

Reflective activity

Representations of what constitutes a 'proper family' are everywhere in the mass media and form powerful images in children's literature and in the minds and discourses of the adults who teach, care and take responsibility for children. However, children's understandings of what family means to them in their own lives are often broad and inclusive . . . children and young people include within the rubric of the term 'family' their parents, siblings, grandparents, step-parents and step-siblings, and their uncles and aunts, but they also include pets and people not usually considered as kin. [A] study of 8 to 11-year-olds suggested that children's definitions of what counts as family become more complex as they grow older.

(Brannen *et al.* 2000, p. 47)

Consider what Brannen and colleagues (2000) say about how families are portrayed in the media and in your setting or school. Do you see representations of a wide range of 'families' or do they all seem to fit the nuclear family model?

Think about activities you might devise to enable children to explore and celebrate who they see as being part of their family.

Attachment and attachment disorders

In Chapter 1 we explored how children need to form secure attachments with those who care for them. We have also discussed 'how easily attachments can be disrupted' (Raicar 2009, p. 79). These attachments may be disrupted by families breaking down, through separation and divorce, or by a family becoming splintered through the need to seek refuge or asylum. Subsequent chapters in this book will also explore how family breakdown may occasion the need for children to become children in care (CiC), or tragically children can lose primary attachment figures through the death of a parent. Some children who have never had the opportunity to form appropriate attachments or who suffer trauma through disrupted attachments can go on to develop attachment disorders. Early years settings and schools need to be aware of the signs a child with an attachment disorder might display in order to know how best to support that child.

Pearce (2009) and Archer (2003) discuss how if infants have been unable to form necessary attachment bonds in their first 6 months of life they may grow up to be children and young adults who display long-term attachment disorder with symptoms such as 'depressive, dissociative, eating, identity and personality disorders' (Archer 2003, p. 79). In some cases these children may grow up to self-harm, or to have eating disorders or suicidal thoughts or tendencies (Cooper 2007), and where help and support has been provided at some point to help such children there can be lapses into previous behaviours at times of particular stress. Controversially Pearce (2009) and Archer (2003) also suggest that 'poor, inconsistent or traumatic early attachment relationships have been shown to lead to the establishment of very different brain and nervous system structures' (Archer 2003, p. 85). Such children, Archer (2003) suggests, will also exhibit problems with being able to control or manage their behaviour, or to think through things that have happened, or to think about the future in terms of consequences of actions and 'building' a future. They struggle to form mutually rewarding, caring relationships and tend to seem to 'live in the present'.

Secure, caring early attachments are so necessary to enabling a child to thrive as they are part of what gives a child a sense of self, and a self that has worth; that is, that they are important to those around them and therefore important for their own sake. Where attachments develop appropriately and children begin to understand themselves as important, autonomous beings, they can then begin to see others as separate, also autonomous worthwhile persons. If a child does not develop these capacities they do not know how to make judgements between what might be 'good' relationships and 'bad' relationships; they do not have the facility to discriminate between who they might trust and who may prove to be seeking an abusive relationship. For many children who are subject to sexual abuse it is because they have the capacity to be groomed by sexual predators, since they cannot distinguish between appropriate and inappropriate cues as to whom they may or may not trust in forming new relationships. Similarly, they may not be able to distinguish between appropriate and inappropriate attention, as from the child's point of view there have never been any rules as to how to get attention; in their experience attention has been something that does not occur in a predictable, manageable way (Knowles 2009). 'Chaotic–disorganized attachment behaviours are shown by children who have learnt no strategy for keeping themselves safe' (Raicar 2009, p. 33).

Reflective activity

Behaviours that can signal attachment disorders

A child may appear overly anxious or worried. Many children are anxious or worried over things from time to time, but if the child you are concerned about seems worried about most things, particularly those things that other children take in their stride, or if they cannot be comforted and their worries abated, then it is helpful to note this behaviour and consider it alongside other signal behaviours that might be present (see below).

The child may have difficulties trusting other children and adults; for example they may not want to share, as they may not trust that they will actually get their turn, or their part of whatever is being shared. They may be unable to settle to an activity for more than a few minutes or may easily lose concentration. They may be scared of trying new things, including new activities, going to new places or even playing with new toys. They may appear very 'clingy' to adults in the EY setting or school, or be constantly asking after whoever drops them and collects them from the setting or school.

Some children who have attachment disorders may appear very withdrawn and, left to their own devices, seem to do nothing but watch others. If they have an accident they may be unable to seek help or comfort (not knowing that help and comfort is there for them, having not been used to experiencing it). This may extend to not asking for help if they are unsure of learning tasks and activities they are being asked to do.

The behaviours listed above can sometimes go unnoticed as many of them can be passive or 'acting-in' behaviours that do not draw attention to the child, in part because the child is used to not receiving attention. The behaviours that are most often noticed are those 'ranging from "acting out" behaviours such as aggression, non-compliant behaviour, vandalism and bullying' (Cooper 2007, p. 15). These behaviours are usually more noticeable because they tend to impact negatively on the children and adults around. As well as having to support and manage children who are exhibiting signs of attachment disorder, schools can find they have an added challenge in engaging children in their learning since the children may also see no reason to be 'attached' to school. Most children do develop attachments to the adults in EY settings or schools and to other children, and as they grow up understand that there are long-term benefits from attending school. Children who cannot attach may show 'indifference or hostility towards teachers and scepticism about the value of schooling' (Cooper 2007, p. 16).

Again, it might seem we have dwelt only on the negative consequences children may experience from step-families; in reality many children are often more accepting of varieties of family relationships than adults. In part this is because children, depending on how young they are when these life-events happen for them, do not have such fixed ideas of what a biological parent should do, as opposed to a step-parent. However, as children grow up, particularly in this instance in step-families, they may need some help in working out their loyalties and relationships with the adults and siblings that form their families. For children the situation may be more complex than for the adults involved as it is often the children who may, across any one week, move between two families, each family having its own rules and traditions. Children, too, may have two sets of brothers and sisters, for example, each occasioning different relationships. Where children can become increasingly confused in such a situation is where a step-family relationship breaks down; that is, if a biological parent and a step-parent separate. In these instances the child, possibly for a second time, loses part of their family and because of the legal situation surrounding step-parents there is nothing to compel others to ensure a child retains contact with a step-parent or sibling they may be very attached to, but who has now moved out of their life.

One of the challenges for step-families, particularly in the initial stages of their formation, is that all those involved in the 'new' family are moving from a situation where they may have well-worked routines and ground rules as autonomous family groups and are then seemingly plunged into a new 'instant family' situation. The new step-family requires negotiation of rules, boundaries and discussions, and most adults will try and prepare the children and themselves for the changes and challenges that setting out together as a new family brings: a family in which all family members already have their own ideas about family life and its attendant worries, needs and wants. This is a very different process and starting place from the 'nuclear' family, which will have grown from childless adults in a new relationship, through a 9-month pregnancy, followed by the learning process adult carers go through to respond to and care for a new baby or to prepare the baby's siblings for a new brother or sister. Arnaut and colleagues (2000) discuss that despite discussions before re-marriage it is not until the new family is actually in place that the reality of trying to work together begins. They comment: 'parents and stepparents had different values and expectations with respect to raising the children . . . Almost invariably the step-parent's expectations were much higher than the parent's' (Arnaut *et al.* 2000, p. 120).

Loyalty can be a further challenging aspect in negotiating new relationships, in that often members of the new family feel confused about who their loyalties are to: their 'old' family and family relationships and alliances or members of the new family. Children may feel resentful of being 'told what to do' by a new step-parent and they may not wish to share adult attention as well as belongings and space with new step-brothers and sisters. The children involved may also be fairly mobile between the new families of both their birth parents. Some children will be visiting both birth parents on a regular, often weekly, basis, trying to maintain their known relationships with their parents while negotiating the emerging rules of the new family. For the adults and parents involved it can seem like refereeing a game with no rules.

Case study

Janine says:

> It was a second marriage for both me and Jake. I have two boys by my first husband and he has a little girl. Prior to the marriage and moving in together we thought we'd done all the right things – involved all the children, made them part of the ceremony, let them choose how to decorate their rooms, sat down and had long chats, etc. But, wham! The first year was a nightmare. Like, my boys had to share a room, where they'd had their own rooms before and Jake's daughter, Tanya, who mainly lives with her mum, had her own room. But the boys kept saying 'she's never here it's not fair she has her own room and it's always empty'. So I let Sam play in the room and didn't check that it was tidy again and he'd moved all his stuff before the next time she came to stay. She went mad, Jake went mad, Sam went mad, his brother joined in to defend him – I defended my boys . . . things like that were always happening. Then there'd be times when they were all out at their mum's and dad's and Jake and I had time to ourselves and then we'd argue like crazy or be so tired we just crashed for the evening.

Sam and his brother say:

> Yeah, at first it was a bit mad. We both hated Tanya, she cried all the time and made Jake do what she wanted and told lies about us and

---

mum really tried to get Tanya to like her and everything was about
Tanya. We ate the stuff Tanya liked, we went where Tanya wanted to
go, we had to watch Tanya's things on TV. We tried to tell our dad,
but he just laughed and said 'that's just girls'. Then one day we
went to dad's and he'd let his girlfriend's little boy play with some
of our stuff and we were like 'whoa, we're getting it from all sides'.

When a step-family forms it has to go through the process of constructing
itself as a family. Many families develop and evolve over time as adults move
out of them and children are born into them. This allows the members of the
family to take more time getting used to change and finding their place within
the changed family. Step-families have different foundations and need to
address issues of possible loyalty conflicts, finding roles and working out how
to perform old roles in new situations. For example, a child might understand
the role of being a sister, but not necessarily a step-sister (Robinson 1993).

Having explored some of the challenges faced by step-families it can be
tempting to think only of the problems that occur; however, for many adults
and children in these situations the new family can bring almost immediate
relief and benefit. Sometimes children will by default have taken on more
adult responsibility when living in a one-parent-family situation than in a
family in which there are two parents. For some children, having a step-parent
move in can allow them to feel less responsible for the care and emotional
welfare of the parent they have been supporting. Arnaut (Arnaut *et al.* 2000,
p. 123) also quotes parents who say that they were better off financially in the
new situation, and several parents stated that they had learned a great deal and
grown personally from being in a step-family.

Case study

Janine, talking about her family as they began to resolve the initial challenges and find ways of living together, says:

Yes I did go a bit overboard with Tanya at first, but that was also
because she is a girl and I'd never 'done' girls before. It was the
novelty of having another female around and being able to look
at girls' things in shops and stuff like that, it wasn't just because
I thought 'I must get her to like me'. And it was good having her
onside and having a bit of back-up over things, like not always
having to watch action movies, getting Jake and the boys not to
leave wet towels on the floor – or anything on the floor, come to

that. I think once I realised this and could explain it to the boys, stuff like – I always had wanted to go shopping but they never wanted to go, so when Tanya did I had someone to go with – things began to get a bit better, in that area anyway. It was the same with Jake, only the other way round: he'd got kids who would play-fight, do banter and, although it all sounds very sexist and traditional, watch football.

Sam and his brother say:

Yeah, Jake can be all right really. He used to shout a lot at first, but now he says 'look guys it would really help me and your mum out if you . . . whatever'. He's quite good at doing stuff too, sometimes dad is a bit tied-up with his work and things, but Jake'll go out on bikes and play Xbox. Tanya can be quite useful too as she's quite good at maths.

The dominant discourse about families may marginalise the experience of those living in step-families

Case study

Charmaine is in her late thirties. Her parents separated when she was very young. By the time she was 7 her birth parents had divorced, re-married and had children with their new partners. Charmaine says:

When I was very young, about 5, I remember wishing my parents were together. I didn't dislike my step-parents, I just wanted my mum and dad to be together and to live with them as a family. In many ways I liked my step-parents quite a lot and my step-mother was more organised and a more creative cook than my mother and my step-father was funny and more engaged with me as a child, compared to my father. Both my birth parents were very committed to their second marriages and I sort of feel between the two families, something that is more recognised by my step-parents rather than my own parents. In many ways, it's my siblings who I have had lasting issues with; since my siblings have all always lived with their own parents they don't understand that I respond to their families differently to how they do. They think I have divided loyalties, whereas I simply just have more families and 'parents' to consider.

Much of the way wider society, the media for example, portrays families marginalises the large number of families that encompass step-parents and step-siblings. The significant challenge this can be for the child is that there are no easily accessible ways of conveying to others the nuances of the family relationships they have. For example, the situation that is often cited is the making of Mother's Day or Father's Day cards. A child may have contact with both of his or her biological parents, but also want to celebrate his or her relationship with a 'step-parent'. Similarly, for adults who have been step-parented for many years and now have children of their own there is another set of relationships to consider, the step-grandparent. Similarly as step-parents age and require care there can again be a need to re-visit the relationship with the step-parent to 'work out' caring for the step-parent in such a situation. Often, those involved in the situation have no problem knowing how much they care, or who they care for; it is others, outside the family, who do not perceive the closeness of the relationship and what it means to those involved.

Although the parents, both birth and step, who are involved in families may agonise over their role in the family and their relationships with the children in the family, research, including that by Brannen and colleagues (2000, p. 113) shows that, 'no matter what type of household form children lived in, children considered both their birth parents to be very important to them'. This is not to say that children do not care about step-parents or do not have long-lasting, loving relationships with their step-parents but that children, for either cultural or biological reasons, often distinguish between the sorts of relationships they have with their birth parents and with their step-parents. This can even be the case in which 'parents failed children and when children had little or irregular contact with parents as was the case with the foster children in the study, in most cases children continued to love their birth parents' (ibid., p. 114). In many ways the subtlety of the step-child–step-parent relationship can be appreciated only by those who have experienced it.

Case study

Patrick says:

> I was brought up by a step-father. When I was young I had very little contact with my real dad. Looking back now I see I got on pretty well with my step-dad and he probably had a harder time of it than I did, particularly when I was going through the teen stuff of challenging his authority and things. My mum was always concerned that I saw my step-dad as a dad and used to diss my real dad. But, whatever they did I always thought my actual dad was my real dad and special. When I was about 18 I tried to get in to a proper son–dad relationship with my father, but mum was right, he didn't want

to know. I feel bad about it, like a deep sadness and it's something I have to deal with. It hasn't changed how I feel about my step-dad, since I've always cared about him, and will go the full distance for him, he just isn't my dad.

Now, I'm a step-dad, my partner has a baby by another relationship. I keep telling her, it will be OK, we'll be fine, me and the baby will love each other; but it will be different. I'm not her dad, she won't want me to be, we've just got to make sure it works out for everyone and not have rules about who should do what or who should care about who more.

The importance of the extended family

For many children, those in their family they derive much comfort and security from are their siblings, grandparents and aunts and uncles. These members of the extended family can act as strong benchmarks for children finding their feet in a new family. Extended family members have less raw emotion invested in making the new family work and can feel less pressure to 'make things OK', therefore they may be more ready to talk with children about the previous family and absent parents. Such conversations can be very affirming for children since they may have no other resources to hand to 'check out' memories and feelings about how things used to be. In particular, extended family members provide children 'with a sense of continuity and belongingness' (Brannen *et al.* 2000, p. 152).

> Grandparents were important to children in symbolic, practical and expressive ways: in being 'there for them', in providing practical care, notably when children were young or their parents' marriages were breaking up, and they were important to children emotionally.
>
> (ibid.)

The importance of children having contact with these family members is also endorsed by Edwards (2002), who emphasises the sense of stability and continuity these relationships give children, particularly as other relationship are changing and being renegotiated.

Early years settings and schools working with step-families

Many of those working in educational settings will have experience of being in a step-family, sometimes both as a child and as an adult. However, adults in educational settings will sometimes seem to behave as if step-families are not relevant to what happens in the setting or school and the portrayal of families will continue to follow that of the nuclear family. It is also important to remember that, as with all families, no two step-families will be the same so it is not possible to generalise from one person's experience to another's.

Reflective activity

Consider how the EY settings and schools you have experience of have set out to work with and support children in step-families. Review the setting's or school's policy with regard to home–school agreements and relationships.

- Is there clear guidance about who has parental responsibility for various children and how this compares with how the child views the situation?
- Is there guidance on which parent needs to be contacted and how?

As well as the legal situation governing relationships in a step-family, EY settings and schools need to be sensitive to how those involved in the family are managing and developing their relationships and how these challenges may impact on the behaviour of the children involved. Remember that where such situations impact on behaviour a child may become withdrawn and not necessarily exhibit aggressive or unwanted behaviours.

For many parents, as for their children, schools may often be the only place they feel secure, safe and welcome. What happens in school is a known quantity, even the bad bits. Even where parents had a difficult or bad experience of schools themselves, in times of stress they can use their children's school as a place of sanctuary; although when parents arrive at the school that may not be the first impression that they give. Many times when parents arrive at school seemingly angry and aggressive, what they need is to be in a safe place to vent the frustrations of the wider situation they are trying to manage. Where schools have good home–school relations they will recognise this and deal with such situations accordingly. For example, many schools will have appropriately trained teaching assistants who manage home–school links, providing someone to talk to in times of crises, who can act as facilitators to put parents in touch with wider support services and who usually provide the very down-to-earth, but important, services of a weekly time to meet and have a coffee. Such support for parents such as Janine, above, provides a place for them to meet with others who may be going through, or have gone through, a similar experience. They give parents the chance to 'off-load' and help them remember that they can begin to survive the immediate 'stress by looking towards the future and trying to strengthen their own relationship with their partner in the present' (Arnaut *et al.* 2000, p. 123). Such support also helps the parent feel less isolated and helps them realise they are not the only ones going through such an experience. Talking to others also helps 'normalise' the situation and helps the individual tease out the dynamics of the personalities involved. That is, all families have their challenges; and the challenges being faced by the step-family may be due to the fact that they are a family and not necessarily because they are a *step*-family.

Reflective activity

Immediately after a divorce parents are concerned with effects on the children. They will be concerned about the children's upset at losing their family. They may also be particularly worried that the children may want to live with the other parent, or that they will lose contact with the children (Arnaut *et al.* 2000).

As we have already seen, child–adult relationships work both ways. Although there is a tendency to think of the adults as being in control of the situation, in reality parents' lives and feelings are deeply connected to those of their children. Most parents derive huge emotional support from their children and children give their lives structure and meaning. Where a parent has been 'left' or betrayed by a partner they may appear overly protective of their children to spare the children further hurt. They may seem overly 'clingy', since the parent too needs the comfort and reassurance that their children are not going to leave or betray them too. The situation may be exacerbated where there is conflict and possibly actual or threatened violence surrounding the situation.

It may be helpful for your setting or school to consider some training to help support parents in these situations. Having a policy or strategy for such situations will help those working in the setting or school know how to better support the parent of a child who is going through a difficult situation.

Having the opportunity to discuss such policies, as a staff group, can offer protection to the staff too, as without clear guidance on what to do in such situations members of the setting and school staff can sometimes find themselves more involved in situations than they want to be, or than they are professionally required to be.

6 Gay and lesbian families and gay and lesbian parenting

Radhika Holmström

This chapter explores:

- the background and the facts of lesbian and gay parenting;
- surrogacy, artificial insemination and adoption;
- working out roles and relationships in lesbian and gay families;
- dealing with other people's assumptions, discrimination, the legislative framework and civil partnerships; and
- openness versus privacy and how families choose to live their lives.

The actual shape of families where the parents are gay or lesbian will vary hugely, perhaps even more widely than that of other families. Some children of gay or lesbian families perceive their family arrangements and/or parental sexuality as a 'problem' for other people; others take it very much as the norm. To some extent this depends, also, on the geographical location of the family. In some areas gay/lesbian families will be unheard of, although in other areas there may be several children from such families in the school.

To some extent, lesbian and gay parenting has had much more of a profile in recent years, with people such as Elton John and the *Glee* actor Jane Lynch becoming parents through adoption or (gay) marriage. However, there is still a lot of misunderstanding and/or assumption around this whole topic. This chapter explores the rise in openly gay parenting; the background issues of discrimination, perceptions of lesbian and gay people and the legislative framework, including civil partnerships; the ways in which parents may want or not want openness or privacy about their sexuality; and the assumptions and prejudices among the wider school community, including those which may be held by the staff in the school.

Reflective activity

What sort of issues do you think may be relevant to families where the parent(s) are lesbian or gay? Do you think children from these families face any specific problems – either as a result of their parents' sexuality, or because of the way other people treat them? Do you think children in this situation lose out? Is it 'not fair on them'?

Write down a list of the advantages and possible disadvantages of gay/lesbian families.

If you are a gay/lesbian parent, or someone who has gay/lesbian parents, you may also like to think about the misconceptions that others have had about your family.

Lesbian and gay parenting: the background and the facts

There are no figures on the number of lesbian and gay families in the UK. It seems fair to assume that the number of families is dramatically on the rise and that the number of parents who are happy to be open about their sexuality is also on the rise, as attitudes to lesbian and gay people become (mostly) much more tolerant.

There always have been lesbian mothers and gay fathers in the UK, but until relatively recently most of them kept this very private. It is still the case that parents who are concerned about their children's sexuality tend to put 'missing out on children' as one of their major worries for their sons or daughters. In practice, most of those lesbian and gay parents were people who had produced children in previous heterosexual relationships.

From the 1970s and 1980s on, more lesbians and gay men have actively chosen to become parents, using a whole range of options from donor insemination to surrogacy or adoption. Often, those parents make the choice to co-parent within a relationship (just as heterosexual couples do) and the non-biological parent is as much a parent as the biological one. Legally, the Human Fertilisation and Embryology Act 2008 granted lesbian couples equal rights as parents and same-sex couples are now welcomed as adopters.

Donor insemination

This route is often taken by lesbian women (some people still term it 'artificial insemination'). At its simplest, it involves taking sperm donated by a male friend and inserting it into the woman's body using some kind of syringe (this is where the cliché of 'turkey-baster babies' comes from). These days, quite a lot of women use fertility clinics in which the sperm has been donated anonymously. However, since 1 April 2005 anyone who donates sperm (or eggs or embryos) can legally be identified by any children conceived as the result of this donation; when they turn 18 they are entitled to request and receive their donor's name and last known address. Donors who donated before 1 April 2005 are automatically anonymous. This means that donor-conceived people can access only non-identifying information provided by the donor at the time of donation, unless the donor has actively chosen to remove his or her anonymity.

Not all women using donor sperm (or eggs or embryos) are lesbians; they may be using sophisticated fertility techniques such as in-vitro fertilisation (IVF) or intracytoplasmic sperm injection (ISCI) in order to conceive. Otherwise, women make different choices according to their circumstances. Some are conceiving with the assistance of a specific male they know, whether he will or will not be involved in the parenting and upbringing of the child. Others do not have a specific donor in mind, and/or they want to ensure that the sperm they use has been screened for sexually transmitted infections and also for some genetic disorders. The Human Fertilisation and Embryology Act 2008 and the Civil Partnership Act 2004 have made it easier for lesbian couples to secure parental rights for any children they conceive through donor insemination.

Case study

Fiona and Annie have been partners for 7 years, and have two children, Maisie and Joe. Both of them always wanted children, and soon after they got together they started discussing the issue of babies and who would give birth to them. They wanted at least two children. Because Annie had a steady, well-paid job and Fiona worked as a freelance designer, they decided that Fiona would have their first baby. They did not have a donor in mind, so decided to opt for a clinic route, particularly as they did not want at the time to involve other people in their parenting arrangements. Maisie was conceived after 6 months of using the clinic; both parents went to antenatal classes together, and Annie's employers gave her the same amount of parental leave as they would give a man whose partner had given birth.

Two years after Maisie was born, they went ahead with a second baby. Originally, they had assumed that this would be Annie's 'turn', so that they would both get the experience of pregnancy and breastfeeding. In the event, though, they decided that this would not be ideal for their particular family set-up. By this point Fiona was fairly settled into a mix of childcare and part-time design work, while Annie was working in a very full-on full-time job. In addition, Fiona had very much enjoyed pregnancy and wanted to do it again, whereas Annie found that, although she very much wanted another child, she did not necessarily feel a huge urge to go through with 9 months of pregnancy, childbirth, and then another six or so months out of the workplace. They opted for the clinic again, initially using sperm donated by the same man whose sperm they had used for Maisie, but then a few months later moving on to sperm from a different donor. Joe was conceived after a year and is now 3 years old.

Maisie and Joe live in a very stable, nuclear-style family with two involved parents, one of whom works full-time and one who works part-time, but who both spend a lot of time with their children and share childcare and housework pretty equally during the time when they are both at home. They call Annie 'mummy' and Fiona 'Fi'. Annie's parents live nearby and babysit at least once a week. Fiona's family is further away but her parents visit regularly. Maisie and Joe are treated, by both sets of grandparents, in exactly the same way as their other grand-children. Fiona is listed as 'parent' on all contact lists alongside Annie. Other people, however, do question their family from time to time. Fiona's sometimes asked whether she wants any children 'of her own' (to which she always responds 'I've got two, thank you, one girl and one boy'). At Maisie's school and Joe's nursery some of the staff have asked about 'the children's mummy' when Fiona drops them off or comes to collect them, and/or ask if she is their 'auntie', even though they've met her at parents' evening.

Adoption

It has always been legal for lesbians and gay men to adopt as individuals, in the same way as heterosexual single people. Since 2005, it has been legal for same-sex couples to adopt jointly, in the same way as heterosexual couples, and a growing number of couples are going down this route. Most local authorities welcome lesbian or gay adopters, and adoption agencies that refused (usually on religious grounds) to extend their services to same-sex couples have had to close.

Adoption is not an 'easy option' for any prospective parents (see Chapter 8). Would-be adopters have to go through a lengthy process of clearance and training before they are in a position to take on their new child. Almost inevitably, as well, the child they adopt will have gone through some extremely difficult experiences – this is the reason why children come into the care and adoption system in the first place. Adopted children often have had to live through far more than other children. Many children feel extremely conflicted about their birth parents, however badly they were treated. Many children present with some degree of 'attachment difficulties' because they have had such a range of different carers in their lives (including periods when they had no effective carer) before becoming adopted. For lesbian or gay adopters, this is compounded by all the other assumptions and prejudices that people, including birth parents and sometimes foster parents as well, may harbour about their ability or right to become parents.

Reflective activity

In an article headlined 'Family in 11th-hour legal battle to halt brothers' adoption by gay couple', Reid (2009), writing in the *Daily Mail*, describes the following situation of the extended family of two young boys protesting to Somerset Council that they do not want the boys adopted by a gay couple.

'The grandparents, an aunt and an uncle have all offered to give the boys, aged six and nine, a loving home but they say social workers have turned them down without explanation' (Reid 2009). The boys' grandparents stated that they were not homophobic, but that having their grandsons adopted by a gay couple was against their Christian beliefs. It is also reported that their grandmother stated that: 'Our grandsons are being forcibly taken from a family who want them dearly. We are worried they will be indoctrinated into a different lifestyle. This is social engineering by the state' (ibid.). The boys had been taken into care as a results of long-term family issues to do with post-natal depression and domestic violence and despite a number of family members coming forward saying they would care for the boys 'the boys have been sent to two different foster homes in two years, which their mother says has coincided with a number of emotional problems' (ibid.).

A spokesman for Somerset County Council said: 'We cannot comment on individuals. However, all our cases go through a lengthy legal process. All stakeholders are consulted and the final decision is made by the judge' (ibid.).

Reflecting on the issues raised by this case, consider: whose needs are of primary importance here and why is the issue of the adopting couple's sexuality the focus of attention?

Case study

Jamal and Martin adopted their daughter, Natalie, last year when she was 3 years old. Jamal has always wanted children – he comes from a big family and one of the hardest things for him to come to terms with about his sexuality was the prospect of remaining childless. It was less important for Martin – he had never thought much about children when he was younger – but when the two of them first got involved Jamal made it very clear that, as far as he was concerned, any long-term partner had to accept that they would have a family. Initially they discussed co-parenting with a single woman friend of theirs, who then met someone else and decided to have a family with him; and then they started the long process of adoption. They were very clear that they were prepared to adopt a child over baby age, and, as Jamal is from an Indian family and Martin is white Scottish, they were also considered appropriate parents for a child of mixed Asian/white origins.

Natalie had been in care since she was 18 months old. She took some time to settle in with her new parents; she is not a very secure child, and she needs a combination of secure boundaries and a lot of reassurance when she is 'naughty'. She is now very happy with her two daddies (she calls them Daddy Jamal and Daddy Martin) and has started in pre-school.

Jamal's family have been very happy about his new daughter. One of his brothers lives very nearby, and his older children have been thrilled to meet their new cousin and treat her as a new and rather lovely small sister. (In fact, it is this feeling of being part of a big, accepting and loving family which has been particularly significant in making Natalie feel relaxed and happy after her very stressful early years.) Martin's family have always been much less happy about his sexuality in general, and his father in particular refuses to talk about it with him. When he announced that he and Jamal were adopting, his father simply ignored him, while his mother and sister were obviously uncomfortable talking about it. So far they have made excuses when he has invited them to see his new daughter, and he keeps suggesting it only because he is very angry at their attempt to ignore this central part of his life.

At pre-school, the staff and most of the parents know that Natalie has two daddies. Some people (including one or two staff members) do snigger about this behind Jamal and Martin's back; others have said, occasionally, that they think this is 'wrong'. On the other hand quite a lot of fellow-parents have been extremely relaxed about this and one pre-school worker pointed out that, as she is a lesbian herself, this is hardly an unusual situation for her. The main problem is that Natalie does have some behavioural problems: she is very easily upset and can escalate to throwing things and hitting other people . People tend to attribute this to her family situation and the idea that her fathers 'can't handle her', rather than anything else (such as the things that may have happened to her in her birth family).

Surrogacy

One other option is surrogacy and since 2010 it has been legal for two gay men to be named as parents on the birth certificate. However, this is not, at the time of writing, a particularly widespread or popular option for many gay men.

Reflective activity

Re-read the two case studies above. If Maisie, Joe or Natalie were a child in your class, do you think there would be particular issues you might need to think about, either in treating them individually or in your approach to the whole class?

You might want to think about:

- watching out for bullying or name-calling from other children;
- attitudes among other parents;
- other children asking questions about the three children's families and how you might want to handle this;
- colleagues asking you about the children's families;
- things that Natalie does, or says, which may be the result of other things in her past (see the adoption chapter);
- support that Natalie's fathers may need in dealing with Natalie's issues – as opposed to their own sexuality and family set-up; and
- how you, and others, react when the children talk about their wider family, such as their grandparents (especially when Joe and Maisie talk about Fiona's family): do you consider those their 'real' grandparents?

There is not necessarily a 'right' or 'wrong' answer to all these points; a lot also depends on how the individual family wants to be treated (and there is more on this below). However, these are issues that are useful to think about.

Working out roles and relationships in lesbian and gay families

Some families, such as the two examples cited above, operate with a two-parent model. Others involve a whole range of different people. In some families there may be, for instance, two lesbian parents, a biological father and perhaps his gay partner as well: and those men might either be active co-parents or still have a role which is rather different in the child's life.

Case study

Jenny and Moira have two sons: 5-year-old Isaac and 2-year-old Daniel. Isaac's biological father is a (heterosexual) friend of theirs called Max, who now lives in Hong Kong. From the beginning, they all agreed that Max would have a fairly hands-off involvement with the baby; Max does not want to be a father but, as a long-standing friend of Jenny's, was very happy to donate sperm on the basis that he would not play any kind of parenting role. He does visit, and is finding that he enjoys spending time more and more with Isaac as he grows up. As far as Isaac is concerned, he knows that Max is his 'bio-dad' and he too enjoys seeing him (this may be partly because Max always brings them all, including Daniel, presents), but he does not think of him in any way as a parent.

Max had moved abroad by the time Jenny and Moira were thinking about their second baby, so it was not feasible to ask him to donate this time round. They had also, by this time, got to know a gay male friend called Simon, who was keen on having some kind of fathering input (although not necessarily a full-time parenting role), and he was happy to donate. Simon comes round quite regularly, and has both boys round overnight occasionally. They are all still working out exactly what his role is. He is currently single, but does not want to commit any potential partner to parenting; at the moment it works well, and they are all happy with it.

Case study

Paul and Nitin, and Kathy and Miranda, have two children. Paul and Nitin live round the corner from the other couple, and 4-year-old Mariam and 3-year-old Aisha divide up their time fairly equally between both sets of parents.

Paul and Kathy are Mariam's biological parents, and Miranda and Nitin are Aisha's. They always had this in mind; they all wanted children, they have known each other since university days, and they decided some years ago that this would probably be one of the most practicable ways to have children.

In many ways, this works very well. The children certainly consider that they have four parents, and although they are not biologically related they are very clear that they are sisters. They also get a lot of input from four parents who are not as exhausted and pressed for time as those in a nuclear family. On the other hand it does mean that any parenting decision is quite unwieldy: all four parents have their own opinions, for instance, on the school that Mariam will go to next year. It also means that any plans to move or go on holiday have to be worked out quite carefully – so far they have all moved once, and sometimes they go away as separate four-people families and sometimes as a full six-person one.

Comment

When it comes to the legislative framework, it's important not to fall into the assumption that partners equal parents. There are two different things going on here. Yes, there's the issue over civil partnerships, etc. But that's entirely separate from issues over parenting. Two women can be in a relationship but not necessarily co-parents: as I and my partner were for our son's first year. Or there might be a whole pack of co-parents involved, like my neighbours, or I've got friends where parents include people who were, but are no longer, in relationships with each other, but not current partners. Or co-parents who are friends.

So following on from that there's stuff over parental responsibility – who has it legally, who's a de facto parent but without parental responsibility, who is the partner of a parent but not a parent themselves. Which can end up with bizarre form-filling experiences where there just aren't the right boxes to deal with.

(Lesbian mother of two)

Some of the assumptions about same-sex families are compounded by assumptions that a biological parent will be the 'real' parent, and/or that the parents will divide up their roles in the same way as very traditional heterosexual families. In practice, parenting roles can divide pretty traditionally (in that one parent will do more of the hands-on parenting while the other goes out to work), or they may be quite fluid. It is important that EY practitioners do not make those assumptions.

Furthermore, similar to heterosexual parents, lesbian and gay parents can also separate and have similar discussions and dilemmas about residence and access to those of heterosexual families. Children whose same-sex parents have separated should not be assumed to live solely with their biological parent, or to feel this separation any less than other children going through similar experiences with heterosexual parents.

Reflective activity

Look at the examples above. If Jenny and Moira's son Isaac were in your class, and his parents separated, think about the way you might want to talk about it with Isaac or with his parents. Think about:

- notes home;
- parents' evenings;
- school plays and performances; and
- contacting his parents to discuss any problems Isaac might be experiencing at school.

Now think about Jamal and Martin, neither of whom is biologically related to their daughter, but who are both adoptive co-parents. Do you feel differently about how they should be approached if they separate? Does the impact of the adoption have any bearing on this?

Finally, go back to Fiona and Maisie. Unlike the case of Jenny and Moira, you know who is the biological mother here, and how the parents have shared out their time, with Fiona working full-time and Maisie part-time. If they separated, would you think about them differently: as one as the 'real' mum and one not?

What about the situation where they may take up with new partners who may or may not want to play a co-parenting or step-parenting role?

Unlike some of the exercises in this chapter, there *are* some 'right answers' here in that all the parents involved are still parents, just as heterosexual parents remain parents, and are struggling to put their parental responsibilities above their personal relationship traumas. They all love their children and want to remain involved in their lives. Equally, those traumas will inevitably have some impact on their children (however much they seek to minimise them) and should not be trivialised. Fiona may not have given birth to her children, but if she moves out they will feel it as much as any birth children would. Jamal and Martin's adoption, and/or their sexuality, in no way diminishes the huge commitment they feel to their daughter.

Dealing with other people's assumptions

There are many widespread (mostly negative) assumptions about how growing up with a lesbian or gay parent, or within a family with two same-sex parents, will affect the children. Look at the list you made for the first reflective activity in the chapter: it is likely that it will include something along the lines of 'lack of a role model for boys' and/or 'other people's prejudices'.

There has not been extensive research into the outcomes for families with lesbian and/or gay parents, but overall the findings suggest that 'children with lesbian or gay parents are comparable with children with heterosexual parents on key psychosocial developmental outcomes. Children with lesbian or gay parents have similar experiences of family life compared with children in heterosexual families' (Tasker 2005). However, those experiences are *compounded* by other people's assumptions about the family and/or homophobia. So in other words, other people's beliefs that 'the children will be worse off' are, in effect, making the children worse off.

Other research backs this up: that it is not the being in the family per se that can cause children distress and/or disadvantage, but the pressures and prejudices that being in that family exposes a child to. So, by extension, it is at least partly the job of the EY setting to nurture an environment in which having gay parents is straightforward and accepted. It is significant, in this respect, that at least one school-based survey conducted in the UK found that, although students with lesbian parents did not report differently from students with opposite-sex parents (or from the general student sample), in relation to victimisation, children of lesbian parents were less likely to draw on school-based support through services such as school teachers, nurses and counsellors (Rivers *et al.* 2008).

Reflective activity

Martin is in your reception class. He is 4 years old. He has two parents, both women, called Tricia and Melanie. They separated when he was 2, and he now spends some of his time with Tricia – who has a new partner – and some of his time with Melanie. Both parents have made big efforts to minimise the effects of their separation on Martin; however, it is clearly having an impact on him.

Martin has some friends in class. However, one of his best friends, Layla, has parents who do not let her go to either of Martin's homes, and do not want to invite him round either. When asked they say they have 'nothing against' Martin's home background, but they do not seem to have any problems with inviting anyone else round after school. Another parent, the father of Martin's friend Jack, seems to be equally set on not letting his son invite Martin round, although so far nobody has questioned him on this.

Martin is clearly unhappy about quite a lot of things. He does not want to talk about them, but it is obvious that he is feeling confused and does not know how to cope. He can find ordinary things in class, such as being asked to sit down at story time, or join in with a group activity, very difficult from time to time. Occasionally he goes into 'meltdown' in class, bursting into tears and/or getting very angry with other children. At other times, when he is happy and relaxed, he is an extremely easy-going child who gets on well with other children.

Think about some of the reasons people might give for Martin's behaviour. Please note that this is not just the reasons *you* might give, but the opinions other people might have. They might include:

1   social isolation because nobody knows how to talk to his parents;
2   lack of a father figure;
3   inadequate parenting because his parents are both women;
4   inadequate parenting because his parents have split up;
5   embarrassment about his own family structure;
6   unhappiness because his friends do not invite him round;
7   confusion because his parents have split up;
8   unhappiness because other parents seem uncomfortable around his parents;
9   confusion about his own family structure.

In reflecting on your responses to the issues raised above, think about which of the reasons given are based on *other people's treatment* of Martin and/or his parents, such as points 6 and 8; which ones imply that *there is a problem* with Martin's family because his parents are both women, such as 2 and 3 above; and which have nothing to do with his parents' sexuality. Some, such as point 1, could be interpreted in different ways: is the problem of social isolation because other people have a problem with Martin's parents, or should Martin's parents have 'known better' when they had children in the first place? (This is rather like the argument that people of different ethnicities should not have children, because it's 'not fair on the children'.)

Now think of some of the ways you might want to tackle the situation. Are there ways in which you can find some time and tactics for getting Martin to explain what is bothering him? If you talk to his parents (bearing in mind that they are *both* his parents, whether or not one of them is also his birth parent) how do you want to phrase it? Do you want to talk about the effects of the separation, or about the concerns you have that other parents are being homophobic? What about talking to the parents who are refusing to let their children play with him? Are there stories, games or exercises you can do with the entire class that endorse the point that families come in all kinds of variants, including families similar to Martin's? Some of this is going to depend on Martin's parents themselves, and how far they want their family arrangements and sexuality made the subject of open discussion. However, it is the school's responsibility to ensure that Martin feels safe and happy and able to learn, so it is important for you – and, clearly, your colleagues – to think about how this can be made possible.

Discrimination and prejudice

It is now illegal to discriminate against people on the basis of their sexuality; however, that does not mean that lesbian and gay parents now automatically live in an atmosphere of general tolerance. There is still widespread prejudice, in particular, about the 'right' of lesbians and gay men to become parents. However, the overall climate of tolerance towards, and openness about, single-sex relationships has changed enormously over the past century. Many lesbian and gay parents are legally recognised as partners, through civil ceremonies. And for many people sexuality is no longer regarded as a purely 'private' issue; it is considered an intrinsic part of identity and lifestyle, and one that also does not preclude becoming a parent.

However, those attitudes, and that legal protection (which in practice may not mean very much, in any case) are extremely recent. Sex between men, in particular, was illegal in the UK until relatively recently, and remains so in many parts of the world. Sex between women is less explicitly criminalised; however, that is not because lesbianism is more widely accepted, but part of a reluctance to believe that women might have an active sexuality at all. 'Buggery' was punishable by death in England and Wales until 1861, and remained illegal until 1967, when the Sexual Offences Act decriminalised homosexual acts between two men over 21 years of age and 'in private'. It was decriminalised in Scotland only in 1980, and in Northern Ireland in 1982. The age of consent for gay men in England and Wales was levelled to 16 (the same as for heterosexual couples) only in 2001.

In other words, most gay men of parenting age in the UK grew up in a culture where expressing their sexuality was, at least at some point, not just socially condemned but actually illegal. The Equality Act 2006, which established the Commission for Equality and Human Rights and made discrimination against lesbians and gay men in the provision of goods and services illegal, gained Royal assent only on 16 February 2006.

The changes were made possible only as the result of continual, often very courageous, campaigning on the part of lesbian, gay and bisexual activists. The late 1960s and 1970s saw a time when gay men and lesbian women started talking openly about their sexuality, and about their rights not just to a sex life but to a love life and openly expressed relationships and families; for example the campaigning group Action for Lesbian Parents was set up in 1975 after three high-profile cases in which lesbian mothers were refused custody of their children. The rise of 1970s feminism, in particular, drove some of this; although by no means exclusively lesbian, it enabled women to assert a lesbian sexuality much more openly, and with the support of other women (lesbian or not).

This has also forced a shift in the general attitudes towards gay sexuality. Although there are certainly circles, including in the UK, where it is still considered unacceptable, 'wrong', and possibly an indication of psychological disturbance, overall there is a much wider acceptance of lesbianism and homosexuality. According to the 2010 British Social Attitudes Survey carried out by the National Centre for Social Research (www.natcen.ac.uk/study/british-social-attitudes-26th-report), the percentage of people surveyed who thought homosexual acts were 'always' or 'mostly' wrong has dropped from 62 per cent in 1983 (when the survey was first carried out) to 36 per cent. However, this is still over a third of the population. As far as same-sex families are concerned, that means that their lives, their lifestyles and their families face a huge amount of prejudice, even if expressing that prejudice openly is now illegal.

When it comes to EY settings and schools, the cases and exercises set out earlier in this chapter clearly demonstrate that children who are perfectly happy with their own parents – and regard them as the norm – can face considerable difficulty with other children and/or parents, and with the wider community (including some of the assumptions and prejudices that staff members may have too). They need support from their teachers in order to be able to talk about their families as openly as other children do. They particularly need teachers who treat their families *as* the norm, and who respect both (or more) parents equally.

In 2010 (Guasp 2010) the Centre for Family Research at the University of Cambridge conducted interviews with 82 children and young people who have lesbian, gay or bisexual parents, to learn more about their experiences, both at home and at school. The study, 'Different Families', found that very young children with gay parents tend not to see their families as being any different from those of their peers. Many of the older children said they saw their families as special and different, but only because all families are special and different, though some felt that their families were a lot closer than other people's families. The report found that children with gay parents like having gay parents and would not want things to change, but that sometimes they wish that other people were more accepting.

Reflective activity

Consider the following comments from Stonewall's report 'Different Families: The Experiences of Children with Lesbian and Gay Parents' (Guasp 2010).

How other people feel about my family

- 'Most people, including friends at school, are fine about children having gay parents. They think it is a good thing, or do not really care. When children are younger though they can be a bit confused and do not understand that someone can have two mums or two dads because their family isn't like that' (Guasp 2010, p. 3).
- Where children are unkind about another child's lesbian or gay family it can often be due to lack of knowledge and understanding or contact with lesbian and gay people.
- 'Children with gay parents like having gay parents and would not want things to change but wish other people were more accepting' (ibid.).
- Often the term gay is used as a general insult in schools. This is technically homophobic abuse and schools need to address the use of the term in this way, just as they would the use of a racist term.
- 'Some children with gay parents find it easy to answer these questions, but others find it annoying and uncomfortable' (ibid.).
- Lesbian and gay families need to be part of the usual day-to-day way families are mentioned and form part of school life – in stories, displays, cards sent home for special occasions and so on.
- If the above is not in place, lesbian and gay families can be marginalised, which can lead to children being bullied, feeling they and their family are invisible, or having no way to discuss with others their family and family life.

The recommendations from the report (Guasp 2010) are that EY settings and schools need to ensure that:

- Both staff and children do not make assumptions about gay and lesbian parents.

- Learning activities and the learning environment reflect the different families children come from.
- Lesbian and gay people are reflected in the curriculum.
- Adults in EY settings and schools respond to homophobic language just as they would to racist language.

Reflective activity

Think about the points raised in the Stonewall report (Guasp 2010), especially the points that schools are not taking homophobic bullying or language seriously and are not supporting children adequately. Is there anything you can do at work to change this, especially the casual use of the word 'gay' as an insult?

Openness and privacy

Most of this chapter has addressed the issue of families' needs to be a public part of the parenting community. Many lesbian and gay parents are very open about their sexuality. It is a matter of pride to them that their children grow up happy to talk about the family they grew up in. They may well feel, too, that parenting makes it even more important to be open and relaxed; they do not want their children to feel that there is something to hide at home.

Other parents may feel differently, especially if they live in an area in which there are very few lesbian or gay parents; they are not necessarily keen to hide anything, but they do not particularly want to turn their sexuality into a talking point.

Early years settings and schools need to respect and reflect both those points while also making it clear that prejudice against lesbian or gay people is unacceptable, and that all children need to be able to talk unguardedly about their home life.

7 Families, disability and mental health

Radhika Holmström

This chapter explores:

* what is meant by the term 'disability' and the family experience of disability;
* having a disability, the medical and social models of disability and discussing disability;
* having a disabled sibling;
* being a disabled parent;
* mental health;
* being a child carer; and
* disability in the family and discrimination, poverty and hate crime, as well as the prejudice experienced by some families.

Disability and the family

Many families contain someone who is disabled in some way. It may be a physical disability, a learning disability or a mental health problem; it may be very obvious to the outside observer, or it may be something that most people do not know about. Whatever it is, that disability does not just affect the one person who has it; time and again, every organisation that works in supporting disabled people makes the point that disability affects everyone in the family to some extent, from the options they have for family outings to the money that is available for school trips. However, it is important not to assume that all those effects will be negative ones. Many people with a disabled relative speak with enormous pride and love about that person. They also say how much they have learned from knowing about disability at such close range.

This chapter explains the issue of disability in more detail; looks at the effects of having a disabled parent or sibling; and talks about the wider issues of discrimination and misunderstanding that disabled people and their families face, in the local community and within wider society.

What is disability?

Disability is commonly thought of in terms of physical disability and wheel-chairs; in fact the term covers a huge range of physical, mental and sensory issues. Some people become disabled as the result of accidents or illness (such as a bone tumour or eye cancer). Some have progressive disabling conditions (such as multiple sclerosis). Some have 'invisible' disabilities, such as epilepsy; others have conditions that sometimes cause them problems and sometimes do not get in the way of daily living at all.

Reflective activity

Make a list of people you would consider 'disabled'. Think about how you define 'disability'. Would you consider someone with very bad sight disabled, or would they have to be registered blind? What about people with facial disfigurements? Do you think people with depression should go on the list or not?

If you are disabled, how do you respond to the way those without disability seek to label people similar to yourself? What would you like people to know about being disabled?

The Equality Act 2010 (http://www.homeoffice.gov.uk/equalities/equality-act/) defines someone as having a 'disability' if:

- they have a physical or mental impairment; and
- the impairment has a substantial and long-term adverse effect on their ability to perform normal day-to-day activities.

For the purposes of the Act, these words have the following meanings:

- 'substantial' means more than minor or trivial;
- 'long-term' means that the effect of the impairment has lasted or is likely to last for at least 12 months (there are special rules covering recurring or fluctuating conditions); and
- 'normal day-to-day activities' include everyday things such as eating, washing, walking and going shopping.

People who have had a disability in the past that meets this definition are also protected by the Act. So are people with 'progressive conditions', that is conditions that deteriorate over time. People with HIV, cancer or multiple sclerosis are protected by the Act from the point of diagnosis.

The definitions of the Equality Act are useful guidelines. They are not the only way of defining disability, and some people would query the language they use (see below). But, importantly, they show that disability covers a huge range of people.

The way we think about disability

The whole picture of disability in the UK has changed beyond recognition in the past century. The first Disability Discrimination Act was passed only in 1995. The Act, and the political campaigning that brought it about, was the result of disabled people making it clear that discriminating against disabled people was as unacceptable as discriminating against people on the basis of their ethnic origin or sexuality.

Reflective activity

Disabled people and their supporters have moved from what is called a 'medical' model of disability to the 'social' model. The disability charity Scope describes it in this way:

> The medical model looks at what is 'wrong' with the person and not what the person needs. It creates low expectations and leads to people losing independence, choice and control in their own lives.
>
> The social model of disability says that disability is caused by the way society is organised, rather than by a person's impairment or difference. It looks at ways of removing barriers that restrict life choices for disabled people. When barriers are removed, disabled people can be independent and equal in society, with choice and control over their own lives.
>
> Disabled people developed the social model of disability because the traditional medical model did not explain their personal experience of disability or help to develop more inclusive ways of living.
>
> (www.scope.org.uk)

In this way, disabled children and adults experience barriers that prevent them from getting on with their lives and having similar opportunities to those without disabilities because of the negative and stereotypical attitudes held by others (ibid.).

Reflective activity

Table 7.1 displays a range of day-to-day situations that illustrate barriers to opportunities encountered by disabled children and adults. Compare the medical model and social model approaches to dealing with these situations. If you are disabled, or have experience of living and working with disabled children or adults, you will be able to think of many more examples in which children and adults have faced barriers to participating in opportunities available to others: barriers that, with very little thought, can be easily removed.

Table 7.1 Comparison of the medical and social model approaches to disability

Challenge	Medical approach	Social approach
A child with mobility challenges who uses a wheelchair needs to get into the building, but there is a step up to the door	The condition that means the child needs a wheel chair is not going to be 'cured', so the child is never going to be enabled to climb the step	Provide a ramp to enable wheelchair access
A teenager with a learning difficulty wants to work towards living independently in their own home but is unsure how to pay the rent (www.scope.org.uk)	Until they learn how to pay rent they are going to be unable to achieve independence and will have to live with their family or other carers	The young person is supported with a strategy that enables the rent to be paid
A child with a visual impairment wants to read the latest best-selling book to chat about with their sighted friends (www.scope.org.uk)	Until the child can see the text, they will be prevented from joining in this activity	The child is provided with an audio version of the book

Reflective activity

Go back to the list about what disability means, which you made at the beginning of this chapter. Are there things you want to add to it, or are there maybe things you now want to remove from the list?

There may be cases where you are still not sure whether someone counts as 'disabled' or not. That is fine; part of the whole discussion of disability is that that people's circumstances change. Some people have conditions that fluctuate from day to day, so that there may be times when they are effectively 'disabled' and other days when they are not and, as the description of the social model above explains, there are times when people face barriers to daily living and times when they do not.

Children with disabled siblings

Inevitably, a lot of time and energy (and often money) is usually devoted to the disabled child, or children, in a family. The other children in the family can feel very conflicted about this. However much they love their brother or sister, they may also feel that their own needs and wants do not come first. They may find it hard to invite friends round to play if their brother/sister has behavioural problems, or the disabled child's care needs dominate the household routines. They may be getting less sleep than the other children in a class, with consequent knock-on effects for their day. They may also find it very hard to talk about their disabled siblings, especially if their parents find it hard to raise the subject as well.

They may also feel that they are expected to behave very differently, and probably more responsibly, than their disabled sibling, even if they are very young themselves; they may feel that they are expected to 'look after' or look out for their sibling. At the same time, they may well love their disabled sibling and feel very protective of his or her needs, meaning that if they do also resent some of the effects of that disability they will feel even more confused.

Case study

Nadia is 4 years old. She has an older brother who has autism. Her brother, Lucas, is in a mainstream class at the school where Nadia is in the nursery, and she sees him in the playground at morning break.

Nadia is a bright, enthusiastic little girl who is doing well. She loves her brother and is close to him. They clearly get on very well together, and if Lucas is upset Nadia is often the only person who can reassure him and calm him down. She does not tend to play with him – he is 2 years older than she is – but if she thinks he is in difficulties she usually drops what she is doing with her own friends, and goes over to find out if she can help. At the same time she is also already finding it hard to explain to her classmates why Lucas behaves in the way that he does, especially if he is behaving in a way that other children think of as 'naughty'. She is finding it hard to fit in with other children as they start to ask each other round to play after school, because she is not sure Lucas would be happy having his home disrupted.

Lucas does not sleep well, and one of their parents usually has to get up to spend part of the night with him. Nadia very rarely gets a proper night's sleep, and she often comes to school looking exhausted, which makes the day very hard for her. Her mother always looks very tired and stressed as well, although she always comes to any parents' events and is keen to support both her children.

Nadia is not unhappy, and she does not think her brother is a 'problem'. They get on very well and she loves being the person who can reassure him when he is upset. However, life with Lucas clearly can be stressful and tiring at times as well.

Case study

Miles is 5 years old and is in reception. He has two younger siblings. His 3-year-old sister, Maisie, has always had various developmental problems, and his parents were recently told that she has a rare genetic condition that results in learning and physical disabilities.

As a result, Miles's parents are spending a lot of time at hospital appointments at the moment. His youngest sister, Tanya, is still only 4 months old, so she also takes up a lot of their time and attention. The household is quite disrupted and Miles is getting confused and unhappy so that it is affecting him at school. He gets very upset when his parents leave him in the morning, and he is demanding a lot of attention from the teacher and teaching assistant. He is spending a lot of time in after school club and breakfast club as well.

Miles's family will get over their current chaos and uncertainty, and find ways to look after all three children, but at the moment he is finding life very hard.

Case study

Izzy is 5 years old and is in reception. She has one older sister in Year 4 at the same school. She also has a brother, Paul, who is at a different school because he has profound and multiple learning disabilities.

Izzy does not talk about Paul very often in class, or not more than most children talk about their brothers and sisters; however, when she makes a picture of 'my family' or describes what they did at the weekend, he is always part of the story. She is making lots of friends at school and does ask them home from time to time. She usually tells them, 'My brother will be at home and he is disabled', or something similar. One other girl did laugh at Paul once, and Izzy slapped her.

Paul goes for a weekend break to respite care about once every 6 weeks. Izzy, her sister and her parents usually do 'ordinary family' things then – such as going to a café for lunch or to the cinema – and those weekends are important to all of them because they can go out and about without constantly having to plan ahead for Paul's needs. It also means that Izzy and her sister get their parents' undivided attention; and it helps enormously to get the chance to talk to her parents about anything that is bothering her (such as the incident with the girl who laughed at Paul).

At the moment, Izzy feels quite uncomplicated affection for Paul and their family life. She is aware that other people's lives are often quite different from hers; however, she does not think of them as 'better' or 'worse'. She likes the weekends without him, but she is always very pleased to see him back in the family again, and she would hate it if he had to go and live elsewhere.

Disabled parents

There is very little research on the experiences of disabled parents generally, and particularly little on the needs and experiences of disabled fathers (Morris and Wates 2006). As children grow older, the assistance parents need may change. The literature that does exist indicates that disabled parents often have particular difficulties with getting their children to and from school, and that within school (and/or similar settings) there are two main barriers: other people's attitudes (see more below) and also physical problems with accessing buildings and/or forms of communication with parents. Schools and other education providers have a duty to disabled parents and must allow 'reasonable access' to services related to the education of their child or children. This is to ensure that disabled parents can be fully involved in their child's education.

This could include:

- providing letters, newsletters and reports in braille, large print, 'easy-read' or on CD;
- using a pen and notepad, or a computer or PDA (personal digital assistant), to communicate with parents who have hearing problems;

- providing a sign language interpreter for meetings;
- updates by phone or email for parents who cannot physically get into the building;
- arranging meetings in accessible rooms (particularly rooms not involving stairs); and
- allowing a disabled parent to be accompanied by an assistance dog.

Reflective activity

Sean is the father of a 10-year-old whom you are teaching. Sean has multiple sclerosis and as a result he uses a wheelchair. He does not speak very clearly, especially when he is tired. He is also a very supportive father who is keen to be involved in his son's education, and he obviously wants to come in for one of the regular updates you hold for parents about their children's progress.

Think about some of the things you might do to make a meeting possible for Sean. Where are you going to hold it? What time of day? Do you need to think about extra equipment for either of you? How much time should you allow for the meeting?

Also think about the *way* you are going to talk to Sean. It can be very easy, if you are not used to talking to people in wheelchairs and/or people with communication problems, to think that you have to speak very slowly and clearly; but there is nothing wrong with his hearing or understanding. In fact, Sean worked until very recently in a rather high-powered job. On the other hand, if he says something you cannot fully understand, what sort of tone and language do you think you should use to ask him to clarify?

Mental health problems

Mental health problems are a separate issue from 'learning disability'. ('Learning disability', which used to be termed 'mental handicap', means a cognitive impairment.) Mental health organisations, including the Royal College of Psychiatrists, estimate that around one in four people (and one in ten children) will experience mental health problems over the course of a year; and that 30 to 60 per cent of people with a severe mental illness have children.

There are a lot of myths, stigma and assumptions around mental health problems, even though they are so common. Epithets such as 'psycho' or 'nutter' are pretty widely used; tabloid (and sometimes broadsheet) coverage of people with mental health issues often depicts them as violent, unpredictable and untrustworthy. This makes it even harder for parents to talk openly about their mental health issues, or children to 'admit' to others that there is a problem at home.

In reality, mental health conditions cover a huge range: from post-natal depression to schizophrenia, and from long-lasting conditions to temporary bouts of illness that clear up relatively quickly. And they clearly affect people differently; moderate depression is less (relatively) incapacitating than a psychotic episode that requires 'sectioning'. But also, many mental health conditions vary in their day-to-day severity, so that someone will have 'good days' and 'bad days'.

Many parents with mental health problems cope well most of the time; but their condition may fluctuate. Inevitably, these fluctuations – the good days and bad days – can make children feel very confused. And the thing that makes mental health problems different from most other disabling conditions is that they actually affect the quality of the parenting, in a different way from a physical condition (even one that puts considerable demands on the child). At bad times, a mental health problem can make it very difficult to function; or it may make it very difficult for a parent to enjoy being with their child and for everyone to be relaxed and happy together, because nobody is secure. It is hard for children sometimes to understand that their parent today – angry, or crying, or unable to get out of bed – is the same person who played with them yesterday. And when someone is having a bad day, it is often hard to do the basic caring work involved in looking after small children (let alone support their education properly), while a more serious mental health problem can put children in genuine danger, especially if the parent is compounding their mental health problems with drugs and/or alcohol.

This is no reason, however, for arguing that people with mental health problems 'should not have children'. Parents with mental health problems love and want to look after their children. They are often scared that their children will be taken away from them – and this worry is well founded, in that childcare social workers estimate that 50–90 per cent of parents on their caseload have mental health problems, alcohol or substance misuse issues (ODPM 2004). And these worries, again, can affect the whole family – especially as many children find it hard, embarrassing or shameful to talk about their parents' illness to anyone else. They may worry, too, that they are going to become ill themselves. Some children withdraw into themselves, become anxious and find it difficult to concentrate on their school work. They may find it very difficult to talk about their parent's illness or their problems, which may stop them from getting help.

Siblings with mental health problems affect the family too, especially if a lot of the parents' attention is on a fluctuating and/or serious condition. This is clearly similar to other 'sibling issues', but again it can be compounded by the specific stigma that surrounds mental health issues (and other people in the family may be embarrassed to talk about it too).

An estimated one-third to two-thirds of children whose parents have mental health problems will experience difficulties themselves (ODPM 2004).

Parents with mental health problems want understanding and support – for everyone in the family. They want:

- help with looking after their children;
- good-quality services to support their children as well as themselves;
- opportunities for children to talk about any fears, confusion and guilt; and
- opportunities for children to meet adults and children they can trust.

Their children also want information that they can understand about their parents' condition, and the chance to talk to other children and adults (though not necessarily formal counseling). (See Social Care Institute for Excellence 2009.)

Reflective activity

Danny started school 4 months ago. It is becoming more apparent that his mother has mental health problems.

Danny's mother has 'good days' and 'bad days'. On good days she is just like anyone else's mother: she is energetic, affectionate and nice to talk to. She reads with him and comes to pick him up from school. On bad days she cannot get out of bed. If Danny or anyone else tries waking her, she either ignores them or starts to cry and tells them to go away. His older sister takes him to school on their mother's bad days and leaves him in the playground before going off to her own secondary school. Her school day finishes earlier than Danny's, so she picks him up on their mother's bad days too.

Danny cannot remember a time when his mother was not like this. He worries a lot about her when she is having a bad day because he does not know whether she will still be in bed when he gets home, or will have made it as far as the kitchen to make a cup of tea. If she is still in bed, Danny and his sister have to keep as quiet as possible and leave her alone. When she is having a good day, he worries every night that tomorrow will be a bad day. Occasionally she will have a good day that turns into a bad day, and on those days he has had to stay late at school in the office till his sister comes to get him because his mother has gone back to bed.

Danny has not told anybody directly about his mother yet. On the days when she comes to school with him, she is perfectly friendly with all the staff, and she came to his end-of-term assembly too. However, the things Danny does say about home are starting to make it clear that there is a problem. When people ask him why his sister brings him to school so often he does say, 'my mother was still in bed'. A couple of times he has mentioned his mother crying a lot. He always looks nervous at going home time. On the occasions when he has had to stay late in the office because his mother had not yet turned up, he became extremely upset but refused to tell anyone why. He also gets very upset if he is given a party invitation or just asked to play at a friend's house, as he does not know what to do. He often puts invitations quietly into the class waste-paper bin.

The first thing you need to do is check with the relevant member of your senior management team about what the EY setting's or school's policy is for such situations. Despite the worries of Danny and his mother, this may be a safeguarding issue that will need the support of appropriate outside agencies. If you come across a case such as this with the children you work with, you cannot solve their problems by yourself.

However, you can think about ways to provide some support for Danny as a child in your class.

- Engage Danny in tasks with you, or a support worker, to give him the chance to chat about anything that is particularly concerning him. There will be very simple things you will be able to do to help Danny, for example finding him a place in school to do any homework or a quiet place to catch up on other activities he enjoys.
- Make sure staff working in the playground in the mornings can keep an eye on him and talk to him when his sister drops him off.
- If appropriate, think of ways to tell his mother quite specific things, for instance that Danny has had a party invitation and that someone else has also had an invitation so perhaps they could take Danny.
- If appropriate contact an organisation such as Mind (www.mind.org.uk) or Rethink (www.rethink.org) and ask for advice about how best to support Danny and his sister.

Case study

Paulette is 8 years old. She has an older sister, Tanya, who is 17. A couple of years ago Tanya started to have periods when she was very withdrawn and unhappy, and recently she got much worse; a couple of months ago she took an overdose. She has been in hospital, and their parents are spending a lot of time trying to sort out what happens now. Paulette has been staying with her grandparents part of the week for the past 6 weeks.

Paulette is very scared and unhappy about what is happening to Tanya. She cannot understand what has happened to her lovely sister and she misses the Tanya who used to play with her and make a fuss of her. She worries whether the same thing will happen to her when she gets to be a teenager too. Her grandparents have not talked much to her about it, and her parents have only said that, 'Tanya is ill but is going to get better', although clearly they are not sure what is going to happen either. She also misses seeing her parents and being a family as they used to be.

In some ways Paulette is also very angry with everyone; her parents for leaving her with her grandparents, her grandparents for not being her parents, and Tanya for 'starting' all this in the first place and taking up everyone's attention.

Child carers

In many families in which someone has a disability, children do some of the caring. Even quite young children can find themselves taking on caring roles of some kind: from doing more around the house than their friends (because of the pressure of caring on adult family members), to help with providing direct care (bathing, toileting, feeding and so on) for a disabled relative. This can be quite minor – 'helping out' with taking someone their medication, getting the towels out while their parent baths a sibling, laying the table and so on – or it can add up to a lot.

At such a young age it is unlikely to add up as much as with some older children; however, caring can still substantially affect their expectations and experience of family life, especially if older siblings are taking on a great deal more. There is a sharp contrast with friends' lives. They may be more tired (quite apart from any disrupted nights from disabled siblings) and stressed. They may well feel under a lot of pressure to behave responsibly, and/or that they are being taken for granted.

Children who have disabled siblings at the same school may find that they are being expected to act as carers there as well, 'keeping an eye out' for their brother or sister. It is very easy for staff to assume that a child who knows their sibling well will know how to explain the sibling's behaviour. However, in practice it means that children with disabled siblings may be put under considerable pressure, and it is particularly important that schools and EY settings do not automatically expect support for disabled children from siblings.

Morris and Wates (2006, p. 71) also make the point that caring roles can have their positive aspects too; they can make it possible for a child to feel that they are doing something for their parent and making them feel better. However, much of the time, children who act as carers do find it quite hard going.

With so many adult responsibilities, young carers often miss out on opportunities that other children have to play and learn. Many struggle educationally and are often bullied for being 'different'. They can become isolated, with no relief from the pressures at home, and no chance to enjoy a normal childhood. They are often afraid to ask for help as they fear letting the family down or being taken into care.

(Clarkson *et al.*, 2008)

Children in the EY age group are much less likely to take on a huge amount of caring responsibility. Yet the 'Young Carers in the UK' 2004 report of young carers noted that 13 per cent of survey respondents aged between 5 and 10 were missing school or having other educational problems (Dearden and Becker 2004, p. 11). Clearly, it is important to keep an eye out for children who may be taking on caring roles, in case this puts them under strain.

Reflective activity

There are an estimated 50,000–200,000 young people in the UK caring for a parent with mental health problems.

- Many of these young people will provide help and support for a parent.
- Some of these young people will be providing care beyond a level that is appropriate for their age; they will be 'young carers'.
- This inappropriate level of care puts young carers' own physical and mental health at risk (Mental Health Foundation 2010, p. 3).

The Mental Health Foundation recommends that schools review their policies to check that the following is in place:

- There is a named person in the setting or school who is responsible for supporting children who are young careers in this position. Part of their role should be to 'maintain active links with young carers' services within the local area' (Mental Health Foundation 2010, p. 6)
- Where a young carer is identified by a member of staff the situation must be handled sensitively. Where possible the named member of staff above 'should then speak to the young carer directly to seek more information about their situation, and signpost them to necessary support networks, possibly including local young carers' services' (ibid.).

- The setting or school needs to ensure it can then 'provide sensitive and confidential support in the school environment, providing pupils with a space to discuss their problems with teachers, school counsellors or peers' (ibid.).
- The setting or school needs 'to provide known young carers with understanding and flexibility regarding coursework and attendance' (ibid.).

Discrimination, poverty and hate crime: the pressures many families face

Despite there being disabled people in extremely prominent positions (including a former Prime Minister with extremely poor sight), there is still considerable stigma in 'admitting' that one has a disability. Although it is now illegal to discriminate against disabled people in the UK, many people who would never dream of discriminating against someone on the basis of their skin colour, gender or sexuality still think of disabled people as 'second class'. In practice, there is still considerable discrimination against disabled people: from taxis that refuse to take guide dogs to venues that remain inaccessible.

At its worst, this discrimination spills over into 'hate crime': instances when individuals or families are bullied, abused and/or attacked. People with learning disabilities, autism and mental health problems are subjected to particular forms of abuse and bullying. Families can live under severe pressure, whether it is a parent or sibling who is disabled.

Day-to-day, families also have to cope with other people's preconceptions about disability. They are not considered to be a 'normal' family, with the same rights to be included as anyone else. At its simplest, for many people, going out of the house as a family means dealing with other people staring, and/or negotiating difficulties that other people do not even notice (such as pavements crowded with other people's bins, which are an inconvenience for most people but far worse for people with sight or mobility problems).

In addition, far fewer disabled people of working age are actually *in* work than the national average; therefore families with a disabled parent are more likely to be living in poverty, and this in itself can have a severe impact on them.

The charity Contact a Family, which surveyed parents of disabled children in 2009, found that:

- Almost 70 per cent of respondents said that understanding and acceptance of disability from their community or society is poor or unsatisfactory.
- Over 60 per cent of families said they don't feel listened to by professionals.

- Over 60 per cent of families said they don't feel valued by society in their role as carers.
- Over 70 per cent of respondents said their child's access to play and leisure specifically for disabled children is poor or unsatisfactory.
- 50 per cent of families with disabled children said the opportunity to enjoy play and leisure together is poor or unsatisfactory.

(Bennett 2009, p. 5)

Families in which someone has a disability often become quite isolated within the wider school community. Some events (such as school trips) may have difficult access. It may be quite hard for a number of reasons to take part in other broadly 'social' activities (from PTA evenings to children's parties).

Importantly, this is not just because of *physical* barriers; it is also because of other people's attitudes. Often this is because other families feel uncomfortable about disability, and would rather not have to deal with it.

Schools and EY settings cannot tackle all the background issues but they can ensure that they strive for as wide an inclusion as possible.

Reflective activity

Having read through the material in this chapter and developed your thinking about the issues raised, think about what is the most appropriate response to meeting someone who:

- is blind;
- uses a wheelchair;
- has difficulty speaking clearly;
- cannot hear you very well;
- walks with the help of a frame;
- communicates only by using a computer or pointing at the letters on a board;
- cannot control their limb movements;
- finds it hard to understand what you are saying because they have a learning disability; or
- has Down's syndrome.

If you have any of the conditions listed above, or a member of your family does, what would you want to tell people about how to respond to you or your family member?

Many children with disabled family members talk about how proud they are of them, and how much they have learned from the experience of living with them. Children love their family and do not understand the problems other people see their family as having. Children want their family to be part of their wider lives, which includes their EY setting or their school, just as other children's families are. It is up to the professionals who work in EY settings and schools to ensure they are not marginalising children or their families because they find it challenging to deal with disability.

8 When family life breaks down

Fostering and children in care

Radhika Holmström

This chapter explores:

- the number of children being fostered or who are in other forms of care;
- the impact of being a child in care on learning and achievement;
- adoption and fostering and supporting fostered children and foster families;
- why children need to be in care; and
- challenges children in care face in the education system.

'Looked after children', or children who are 'children in care' (CiC), are particularly vulnerable in the education system. Most early years (EY) professionals and those working in primary schools will know some of the reasons why this is the case; however, not everyone is aware of the full range of reasons why these children are so vulnerable. It is also often quite difficult to work out why a particular child may be behaving in the way that they are, especially if not all the information about that child has been made public.

This chapter outlines the number of children in public care in the UK today, and the reasons why they come into the care system; the difference between adoption and fostering; the reasons why CiC and fostered children do relatively badly in the education system; the combination of (currently) inevitable circumstances – such as frequent moves between schools – which affect their achievements; and the assumptions and preconceptions other people have about the care system, which mean that CiC are not expected to do well and are not supported to stretch themselves educationally.

The facts and figures

The most up-to-date information at the time of writing shows that the number of CiC is rising: 'according to the Department for Education, there were 64,400 looked after children in England at 31 March 2010: an increase of 6 per cent from 2009 and an increase of seven per cent since 2006' (DfE 2012b). Of these children 43,200 had been in continuous care for at least 12 months, or more. The figures also show that at this time:

- 5,300 of the children were aged under 1;
- 5,600 were aged 1 to 4; and
- 4,500 were aged 5 to 9 (ibid.).

Attainment

The educational outcomes of children in public care are below the national average with only 15 per cent of children who have been in continuous care for at least 12 months gaining five GCSEs at grade C–A*. By comparison, 70 per cent of all those taking GCSEs in 2009 gained five GCSEs at grade C–A*. The figures show that children in the early years and across Key Stages 1 and 2 are also underachieving and that of those children who have a statement of special needs a disproportionally high number of those children are CiC (DCSF 2010c). Similarly, CiC have a higher rate of absence and exclusion than other children (ibid.).

This divergence in achievement between children who are in care and other children continues after school leaving age. Young people who have been through the care system are less than half as likely to end up in education, employment or training as their peers and there is a disproportionate probability that they will be teenage parents. Even more concerning is that the government's statistics show that in 2009 '9 per cent of those looked after children aged 10 or over, were cautioned or convicted for an offence during the year, just over twice the rate for all children of this age' (ibid.). Children in care are also more likely than other children of the same age to be 'identified as having a substance misuse problem' (ibid.).

The difference between adoption and fostering

Fostering is different from adoption. In adoption, a child is legally moved from one family to another; they gain new parents and a new birth certificate and, where adoption is successful, it is permanent (even if their adoptive parents divorce, they are still the child's parents). Fostered children are still part of their original family; their birth parents are not in a position to look after them and they are therefore looked after by foster carers. This may be for any period from a few nights to a number of years. Legally, however, they are still part of their original family; they will have contact with their birth parents and their relationship with their foster carer will often be very different from that which adopted children have with their adoptive parents. It is also the case that fostered children may well be living at quite some distance from their birth home.

Fostering is usually arranged through the local authority; however, it is not all provided by the local authority. An increasing number of independent fostering agencies are now involved in the fostering process. Overall, the term 'fostering' covers quite a wide range of types of care situations, some of which occur for complex, difficult and tragic reasons including when children have to be removed from their families for their own protection. However, children may need to be fostered in the short term for very simple and straightforward reasons, such as if a child's parent is taken in to hospital and social services are in the process of contacting the child's wider family to arrange care for the child. The British Association for Adoption and Fostering (2012) lists the following as being the most common forms of fostering children may encounter:

- **Emergency foster care**, which usually lasts a few nights.
- **Short-term foster care**, which can last up to weeks or months.
- **Short breaks**, 'where disabled children or children with special needs or behavioural difficulties enjoy a short stay on a pre-planned, regular basis with a new family, and their parents or usual foster carers have a short break for themselves' (ibid.).
- **Long-term and permanent foster care**, where (particularly older) children choose to stay in long-term foster care, possibly over years. These children may not be able to return to their birth families but choose to be in foster care until they can be independent adults, rather than be adopted.
- **'Family and friends' or 'kinship' fostering**, 'where children who are looked after by a local authority are cared for by people they already know . . . children can live with their aunts, uncles, brothers, sisters or grandparents without outside involvement' (ibid.).
- Children might be in **private foster care**, which has been arranged by the child's family and, again may be with a close relative. In such cases 'the local authority must be told about the arrangements and visit to check on the child's welfare' (ibid.).
- Children and young people who might otherwise be placed in secure accommodation because of their behaviour may be placed in **remand fostering**. Remand fostering can be done only by specially trained foster carers.

Reflective activity

As can be seen from the list above, there are many different forms of fostering care available, all designed to meet the particular needs of the individual children and families. You may have personal experience of some of these forms of fostering, either as a child who was in foster care, or as an adult involved in fostering children.

Consider the range of reasons children might need to be placed in some of these foster care situations. How children deal with being in foster care will also depend on their age, on why they are in foster care and on the contact they are having with their birth families.

Foster carers

All children in foster care will be looked after by a local authority and the foster carers will work in partnership with the local authority to provide this care. The foster carers may also work with other professionals such as therapists, teachers or doctors to help the child to deal with any fallout from being in foster care. It may also be the case that the children will already have particular emotional, physical or learning conditions and disabilities that will require the support of a range of agencies.

Foster carers are selected through and registered with either independent fostering agencies or the local authority. Some independent agencies operate their own criteria but local authorities welcome applications from people of any age – as long as they are both old enough and physically fit enough to cope with the task – and people from every socioeconomic group. Foster carers do not necessarily have a partner and/or their own children; they may be in or out of work; they may be lesbian or gay, although in Scotland they can foster only as single individuals living on their own; and foster carers do not have to own their own home. Foster carers can also come from any ethnic or religious background. In fact, given what we have already discussed about identity, there has been an active drive to place children with foster carers who reflect and understand the child's heritage, ethnic origin, culture and language.

Foster carers are checked by the Criminal Record Bureau. All applicants attend groups where they learn about the needs of children coming into foster care. Alongside this, they receive visits from a social worker. The social worker will then prepare a report that is presented to an independent fostering panel, which recommends whether this person/family can become foster carers. Training does not stop when a person becomes a foster carer. All carers have an annual review and any training that is needed to ensure they are suitable to continue fostering. Some carers also take a national qualification such as an NVQ level 3 Caring for Children and Young People (or an SVQ in Scotland).

Foster carers also receive some form of remuneration to cover their caring costs. The exact amount depends on whether they are fostering directly for the local authority or on behalf of an agency. In 2011, the charity Fostering Network (www.fostering.net), which campaigns on behalf of foster carers and children in public care, recommends a minimum weekly allowance for fostered children aged up to 4 of £131.47 and £149.76 for children aged between 5 and 10 outside London; in London, it recommends £154.30 for children aged up to 4 and £175.90 for children aged between 5 and 10.

Importantly, many children in care are *not* waiting to be adopted. They have their own families, even though they are not living with them; they may move back to live with their parents. Others stay long term with foster carers who act effectively as family members, but this relationship is separate from the one they have with their parents.

Case study

Sandie is a single woman in her mid-forties who considered fostering in her early thirties, but only took it up 5 years ago when she realised she could now do it as a single person. She now fosters the sisters Yasmin and Anita. Aged 3 and 5 respectively when they arrived initially for a 3-month trial, they are now 8 and 11 and the plan is that they will stay with her long term.

This was an unusually lucky placement because Sandie was able to meet the girls, their mother and their social worker a few days before they moved in. Naturally, though, it has not been without its difficulties at times. 'Neither of them were used to eating regular meals, at regular times. I had to do a lot of work on making it possible for both of them to be used to the idea that you can eat when you are hungry, and eat a balanced diet, and stop when you have had enough.' The children did not know about quite ordinary activities, such as hanging up stockings at Christmas. Even more seriously, Sandie is aware that there was some level of physical and sexual abuse from one of the girls' relatives.

Today, Yasmin and Anita still see their parents and their extended family. Sandie makes it very clear to everyone that she is not actually a relative, however well they all get on; on the other hand, she does refer to the three of them as a 'mini-family' within that bigger network. She is enormously proud of the girls and how well they are doing at school: she has got their 'good work' certificates up on the kitchen wall, along with their own pictures and photos of them in the school play. 'Out there, I'm one of the many professionals involved in their lives. Here, I'm their foster mum.'

Sandie has put a lot of work into fostering; she is no longer working full-time, and she spends a lot of time in meetings and training sessions as well as supporting the girls at home. She is the kind of foster carer that every authority and agency wants to find. In fact, she is looking for a new house at the moment where the sisters can have a bit more room as they get older and start secondary school, as everyone has agreed that the girls have a home with her for as long as they want.

Reflective activity

Think about good practice you have seen in EY settings or schools that supports the learning of CiC. Compare what you have seen with the government's recommendations.

Early years settings or schools should have in place a **designated teacher** who is there to ensure that all CiC in the setting or school have a **Personal Education Plan (PEP)**. As part of the children's PEP it is recommended that they have some **one-to-one tuition**.

A PEP and one-to-one tuition can give the child and the adult working with them the opportunity to fill any gaps in the child's learning experience that may have occurred because of the child's experiences.

For example, most children in a secure home situation will have people at home such as parents, other relatives or older siblings who will:

- be interested to talk to them about what they are doing at school;
- read to them; and
- talk about things they like to watch on television, games they like to play and other activities they enjoy.

Part of the PEP and one-to-one tuition might include *catching up* on some of these activities (DCSF 2009b).

Reflective activity

Children in care can also slip behind in their education through poor attendance. Monitoring attendance and working with foster carers to help the child to feel there is stability and consistency between home and school will help children both settle at school and feel more secure in the foster situation.

Although this may be your first experience of working with foster carers, this may be a child's second or third foster home. It may also be the third or fourth school a child has attended. Such disruption in home life and schooling can have a traumatic effect on children.

Think about working with foster carers, the child and the designated teacher to help build security and consistency for the child. Some of the issues you might need to consider are listed below.

- How often, when and where will you meet to look at aspects of the PEP; where and when will the child feel most secure?
- Making decisions about priorities with regard to academic learning in Maths and English, for example. This does not mean the child needs to be given *extra work* to do, but you can discuss playing

games involving counting, going to the shops to use money, reading with others (not the same as reading *to* others), visiting the library to choose books, choosing comics.

- Making decisions about fun things to do. For example, the child may never have had a birthday party and may not understand about sending out invitations, planning fun food to eat and things to do at the party.
- Is the child interested in football and dancing or are there perhaps other games and activities they may not have had the opportunity to engage with?

Children who have had disrupted lives may need to be taught how to make friends, how to play and how to ask for what they want. They may never have had adults around who have anticipated their needs and wants and, therefore, have no mechanisms for knowing how to approach others and tell them what they want them to know.

Case study

Steffi says:

> I had a very disrupted childhood and was in short-term foster care a couple of times. When I had my first baby the health visitor suggested I went along to the local mothers and toddlers group, which was what they were called then. I was a bit wary of this idea as I didn't know if I would get on with the other mums there. However, I have learnt in life to give things a go. I'd been there for about an hour when it suddenly hit me that these mums were sitting their babies and toddlers on their laps while they were chatting, they were cuddling their children, kissing them on the head, chatting to them, fiddling with their clothes and keeping physical contact with their babies and children in all sorts of ways.
>
> Until then I didn't know you could do that. I didn't know it was normal to want to hold your baby so much and what is more, I didn't realise you were *allowed* to. When I realised this I went hot all over and wanted to cry. Going to that group was one of the best things I ever did for me and my children.

Reflective activity

We have discussed how important it is to have regular contact with a child's foster carers. However, there may be differences in the way you would talk to a foster carer compared with the chats you have with birth parents.

Before you meet foster carers for the first time you might want to talk through with the designated teacher how the meetings might be different and things you want to check out with the foster carers when you meet them for the first time. For example, how does the child refer to them and what do they want to be called? Other things you may need to establish common ground about are:

- how much the foster carer may know about the child's background and how much you should know, or they can tell you;
- how you might talk about any difficulties you are having in class and how you can all work together to support the child;
- areas where you are particularly pleased with the child's achievement.

The background

The main reason why children come into care is as the result of 'abuse or neglect' (Adoption UK 2012). However, children may also need to be placed into care because of parental mental health problems, domestic violence or parents involved with drug and alcohol abuse. Families may have suffered other tragedies, such as bereavements, and be unable to continue to care for their child or children in the short or long term. Some parents place their children in care as, for many reasons, they feel unable to look after the child at that time; some children enter the care system because they are disabled and parents can no longer cope with looking after a disabled child (Adoption UK 2012). However, figures for 2010 show that in England, 'overall, the main reason why social care services first engaged with children who started to be looked after during the year was because of abuse or neglect (52 per cent)' (DfE 2012). This figure was a rise on the figures for the previous year. As Sinclair comments, the current 'care system is very heavily concentrated on children who are at risk of serious abuse or whose family relationships are dangerously fraught' (Sinclair 2005, p. 34). Cleaver (2000) also comments that 86 per cent of children taken into care were already known to social services, in half the cases for at least 2 years before admission, and other research shows that it is likely that between 50 and 90 per cent of children taken into care have suffered abuse (Thoburn *et al.* 2000; Selwyn *et al.* 2003). Researchers considered this figure may be an underestimate, particularly in the case of young children who may not understand or be able to articulate what has happened to them. However, it may also be worth bearing in mind that the same research found in many cases where children were taken into care for reasons of abuse, or suspected abuse, that once they were in care many children did not want to go home.

Challenges children in care face in the education system

Everyone involved in supporting looked after children agree that EY settings and schools play a crucial part in making it possible for such children to flourish. All studies stress the importance of education as a 'protective factor' in ensuring that children do well in future life; not only academically but socially as well. The educational environment can provide CiC with structure in a life that may well have been very chaotic to date, and it is the place in which they meet other children and often keep up with friends from before they entered public care. All those who work in educational settings know that 'children's happiness and social development are at least as important as their academic success' (Sinclair 2005, p. 98) and that the EY setting or school can 'have a major impact on these less academic aspects of life' (ibid.).

Pre-school and EY settings can be particularly important for small children who have experienced deprivation or disadvantage in their baby or toddler years and need additional support with skills such as how to play or interact with other children. However, it is often not easy, either for those children or for everyone else involved in supporting them. The research to date indicates that most children who enter public care are usually behind their peers in academic terms (Skuse and Ward 2003).

Reflective activity

Although the research, supported by the government's own figures, shows that CiC are achieving less well than children who are not in care, the reasons why this is so need some thinking through.

Children in care may not come from a background where they were played with as young children, talked to, read to or through many forms of neglect given the early learning experiences we know children need to be ready for learning when they come to the EY setting or school.

The child's family may have been living in poverty and there are proven links, which we will discuss in more detail in Chapter 10, between poverty or low income and underachievement.

- Children in abusive situations may simply not have had the capacity to engage with and concentrate on their learning.
- Children may have moved around a lot and have had a very disrupted educational experience.
- Children may have been more focused on what was happening at home than concentrating at school. For example, in cases where children come from homes with parents who abuse drugs and alcohol or have health, including mental health problems, children will worry about what they are going home to. They will worry about their parents and any siblings they may have to look after.

Although the figures above (DCSF 2010c) also show that a third of the children who have statements of special need are CiC, the reasons these children may need statements may be very complex and their needs may be very different from those children with special educational needs (SEN) who are not in care. No two children with SEN, whether they are in care or not, will manifest even the same condition in the same way. For example, children who are on the autistic spectrum (AS) will often have a statements of special needs, but not all children who are on the AS will have the same needs; learning needs must therefore be personalised to the needs of each child. With a child who is on the AS there are particular aspects of the condition to be aware of: how the child reacts in social situations, for example. However, this does not mean all children on the AS will react in the same way in all social situations. Similarly, CiC who have a statement of special needs will need to have support targeted to their needs, not necessarily to the fact that they are CiC.

Inevitably, the reasons why they come into care may affect children's behaviour. They may have very little idea of how they are expected to behave in a group. They may not have experienced adult/child relationships in which the boundaries are clearly set and there are sanctions – but not physical ones – for unacceptable behaviour. Children who have been physically or sexually abused may be completely unable to face the idea of changing for PE (Physical Education) or dressing-up activities. Some lessons may be particularly painful for a child.

> Classes where children learn about families and relationships are an obvious area. Others may simply find festive celebrations like Christmas, which tend to centre on the family, hard to handle. Obviously children in care should participate in all these lessons, but teachers should find a way to teach that doesn't leave a cared-for child feeling exposed and singled out.
>
> (The Who Cares? Trust 2012)

Although some children will be relieved at having been removed from their home, they may still be suffering from grief and bereavement (discussed in more detail in Chapter 11). Children may be relieved that their lives are less chaotic and that they are no longer being abused; however, they have still *lost* their home, they may be separated from siblings and they may not know quite basic things about the home or the family in which they are now living.

For around 30 to 50 per cent of children in care, going into care will have meant moving schools. Other children in care who may remain at the same school may now, however, be living in a different area and have to come to school by 'official' transport such as a taxi (Cleaver 2000; Sinclair *at al.* 2004). Being at the same school but moving to a different area will have knock-on effects on friendships.

Case study

A south London headteacher says:

> These are children who have been cut off from all their other relationships and now have to build new ones; often joining a school mid-year, which is difficult for any child, let alone one with this background. Often we don't have the information from their previous school, either. Usually, there'll be behavioural problems too: we're talking about kids who don't know if they can trust adults again, so they're constantly pushing and testing you. They're angry, and they want to lash out.

Standing out

However sensitive EY settings and schools are to the needs of CiC, 'procedure and practice unintentionally mark the children out as different from their peers' (Sinclair 2005, p. 55). Even if the circumstances of the child are kept confidential, CiC almost always stand out from their peers in some ways. They have different surnames from their foster carers, and although in practice schools and indeed other children may not notice this, especially in areas where it is quite usual for different family members to have different surnames, the children themselves may feel acutely self-conscious about this.

Children who are in care may find it very hard to be able to invite other children round to play at their foster carer's home, or to go to other children's houses. There are several reasons for this: they may feel self-conscious about 'admitting' that they are in care; they may assume it is not 'allowed' by their foster carer; their foster carer may have made it clear that this would be inconvenient; and/or they may now be living at some distance from the school and the children who attend it. Whatever the reasons, this is particularly difficult at the EY stage, when social skills and learning to play with other children is a crucial element of the overall 'education' process and when children are too young to make any kind of social arrangements of their own.

Reflective activity

Nina is in care. She seems quite happy and although she can be withdrawn she does usually join in with group activities willingly. Her foster carer, Alison, picks her up by car whereas most of the other children walk, which suggests that Nina is now living some distance away from the school. Nina has several friends that she gets on well with, although she does not seem to be part of the group of children who play at each other's houses at the weekend.

One of Nina's friends has brought party invitations for you to give out to the whole group. Nina does not even want to take one of the invitations and starts becoming distressed.

- How would you support Nina in the short term? What would you say to her, especially as she may not know that *you* know she is in care?
- How would you mention the subject to Alison when she arrives to collect Nina? How would you handle the meeting; would you ask to see her separately, or reserve a time?

Children in care have a whole range of people involved in their lives: birth parents, social workers, foster carers and possibly other practitioners such as mental health professionals. Many of the decisions that are usually very straightforward become very complicated. A discussion of sleepovers or school trips may become subject to a social worker's decision.

Reflective activity

You are organising a trip to the local museum. You are aware that Faisal, one of the children in the class, is in care, although you do not know very much about the background to this. Faisal is usually dropped off by the same foster carer, who is very friendly but is not particularly communicative.

How would you go about raising the issue of the group outing with Faisal's foster carer? Think about:

- Timing – do you need to do this earlier than you would usually let other parents know? Do you need to organise the whole trip further in advance than you usually would?
- Confidentiality – do you need to speak separately to her, and how will you do this?

You want some parent helpers for the trip; Faisal's foster carer might want to come, but you are not sure how Faisal will feel about this. How do you broach this idea with both Faisal and the foster carer?

Expectations and support

> Some families are really funny about the idea of their kids mixing with kids in care, so you probably need to help the child think through how much they tell other people and what they call you.
>
> (The Who Cares? Trust 2010)

The sections above have outlined the extent to which, by the time they enter the care system, many children are at a disadvantage educationally; however they may experience social challenges too as many children are stigmatised within school by the fact of being in care. In 2009 OfSTED reported that nearly half of children in care were afraid of prejudice or bullying, or of being treated 'differently' when people found out about their background. Almost half thought the public saw CiC as bad and uncontrollable, and just under a quarter thought they were seen as troublemakers (OfSTED 2009).

In practice, it may be very challenging to be supportive of a child who is behaving badly in class and who seems to be deliberately disrupting the learning of the class. It may not be easy to engage with a child who clearly has had to live through a great deal and is now inflicting a great deal on other children. If other parents are complaining as well, this makes it harder. However, it is imperative to separate out the different issues involved.

Reflective activity

Luisa is 5 years old. She finds it very hard to pay attention in class, and often gets so upset that she starts throwing crayons and other equipment across the room. She loses her temper with other children too, and resorts very easily to hitting them. With adults, either she is quite anxious and eager to please or she refuses to listen and ignores what they are trying to explain to her. She tends to say very loudly that 'school is boring' if she is faced with any difficulties, and refuses to try any harder.

As her teacher, you are aware that Luisa was taken into care just before coming to your school, and that her family circumstances before she came into care were extremely difficult. It has been made clear to you that Luisa should not be expected to change for PE, and that she is not comfortable with adults making physical contact with her. She is behind when compared with other children, although she is clearly a more able child than some of her achievements to date might suggest. She is particularly happy with any sort of artwork, and was unexpectedly enthusiastic about a recent project involving making an elephant out of a plastic milk bottle. On the other hand, she was obviously confused when she was singled out for doing well; it was very clear that she is more comfortable being told she is 'naughty'.

How are you going to support Luisa, help her deal with the issues she has and support her in getting back on track in terms of her learning achievement?

Children in care present some of the greatest challenges to EY settings and schools. The children themselves may have a number of complex issues that the educational setting needs to support in terms of ensuring the child achieves in their learning. Working with families in the care system can also bring its own challenges. However, these challenges pale into insignificance when set against the positive medium and long-term difference that settings, schools and the care system can make when they work together. As OfSTED (2009, p. 7) reports:

> For some in our discussion groups, being in care had meant getting away from danger: 'being away from mum and dad's behaviour – having a normal life'. The children also said: 'I feel happier because I am away from abuse'; 'living here I'm out of danger'; 'my dad stopped hitting us – I love my foster family'. For other children: being in care could mean 'I get treated a thousand times better'; 'not being scared'; 'not getting beaten up' and 'I have security and love'.

9 Families and adoption

Radhika Holmström

This chapter explores:

- what we mean by the term 'adoption' and what it means for a child to be adopted;
- reasons why children in the UK enter the adoption system;
- who can adopt;
- contact with birth parents;
- inter-country adoption;
- children dealing with loss and forming new attachments; and
- working with adoptive parents and adopted children's experience in the education system.

Adopted children can pass 'under the wire' for some EY practitioners and adults who work in primary schools. Adopted children may well have a stable home and caring parents; it may not even be known that they are in fact adopted. Yet, at the same time, many adopted children do struggle with school, and their parents may struggle too. Children whose present circumstances do not seem to be difficult may in reality be dealing with things that happened to them in early childhood, and those issues may well mean that school is far harder from them to negotiate than a superficial impression would suggest.

This chapter explores how the picture of adoption has changed dramatically in the UK over the past 50 years; the background to adoption today in relation to both children and parents, including inter-country adoption; and the specific issues associated with adopted children's engagement with the education system.

The changing picture of adoption

Adoption used to be the main option for children whose parents both died. It was also the main option for girls and women who became pregnant before marriage – and sometimes after marriage as well – and who did not want to keep their babies. Some went to 'mother and baby' homes to give birth and their babies were taken away virtually immediately. Some abandoned their babies, or had them taken away by relatives. Other parents, including fathers whose wives died, found themselves unable to care for their children and gave them up for adoption later on. As a result, many children entered the adoption system as babies, knowing nothing or very little about their birth parents. Many who were adopted this early did not find out till much later that they were, in fact, adopted. Some found out only after their adoptive parents had died.

Reflective activity

If a child tells you they were adopted, what does this mean to you? Think through what might be their answer to some of the questions you might have – even if it is not appropriate to ask the child:

- At what age was the child adopted?
- Do they know who their birth parents are?
- Have they had any contact with their birth parents?
- How do they *feel* about being adopted?
- Does being adopted cause them any particular problems with school?
- Does being adopted cause any identity problems?

If you are adopted, how do you respond to these questions? Are they intrusive and nobody's business but your own? Are you happy to answer them or mystified that someone thinks they are relevant? What would you like those who work in EY settings and schools to know about being adopted?

Reflective activity

Are there, or should there be, restrictions on who can adopt? Who, from the following list, do you think are allowed, or not allowed to adopt?

- Older people.
- Unmarried heterosexual couples.
- Single people.
- Overweight people.
- Lesbian and gay couples.
- Married heterosexual couples.

- Lesbian and gay couples who have had a civil partnership.
- People living on benefits.
- Mixed-race couples.
- Lesbian and gay couples who have not had a civil partnership.
- Couples who already have children.
- Single parents.
- People who are of a different ethnicity from the child they want to adopt.
- Disabled people.

Adoption today

When a child is adopted, they change family. The child may well have some contact with their birth parents (see below); however, the adoptive family is now the child's family. Legally, their surname changes and the new parents receive an adoption certificate that shows the child's new name and the adopters as their parents. This certificate takes the place of a birth certificate. When the child reaches 18 years of age, they are entitled to a copy of the original birth certificate. This will show the child's original name, as well as the address the birth parents were living at when the birth was registered (www.ukdp.co.uk). Once an adoption order has been granted it cannot be reversed except in extremely rare circumstances.

Thus EY practitioners and adults in primary schools need to be sensitive to the fact that adoptive parents are 'real' parents. They consider their adoptive children to be their own children, and in turn they should be treated as parents, not as carers. Similarly, from the point of view of most adopted children this is their family and their parents.

The numbers

The number of adoptions in England and Wales in 2009 was 4,655. This is a decrease of 5.7 per cent since 2008 and the lowest since 1998, when there were 4,614 adoptions (Office for National Statistics 2012). However, the statistics show that an increasing number of these children are in the EY age group. Almost 60 per cent of children adopted in 2009 were aged between 1 and 4 years compared with only 39 per cent in 1999. The figures also show that the proportion of children adopted aged 1 to 4 has steadily increased over the past decade. Fifty-nine per cent of children adopted in 2009 were aged 1 to 4 compared with 57 per cent in 2008 and 39 per cent in 1999 (ibid.).

In 2009 the proportion of children adopted who were aged 5 to 9 was 24 per cent, the same as in 2008. However, the number and proportion of children adopted aged 5 to 9 has declined significantly over the last decade, from 1,672 children (34 per cent) in 1999 to 1,138 children (24 per cent) in 2009 (ibid.).

Reasons why children in the UK enter the adoption system

As the figures above show, over half the children who are adopted in the UK are still quite young, although they are not babies. Most children have entered the adoption system after a period spent in foster care.

Adoption is different from fostering (see Chapter 8); although the popular picture is of children in care waiting to be adopted, this is not the case for many children. Fostering is usually a temporary arrangement, though sometimes foster care may be the plan until the child grows up. This long-term or 'permanent' fostering may well be the right option for those particular children, because it maintains separate relationships with the foster carer(s) and the family (again this is discussed in more detail in Chapter 8). Fostering does not provide the same legal security as adoption for either the child or the foster family.

It is important to remember that adopted children, who now have very settled, caring families, may have had very different experiences in the past. Chapter 8 outlines some of the reasons why children come into care, mainly as the result of 'abuse or neglect', parental mental health problems, domestic violence, drug and alcohol abuse or what is generally termed a 'chaotic lifestyle'. Other children are placed in care voluntarily by parents who feel unable to cope; a significant proportion of children placed in foster care by parents have a disability which their birth parents feel unable to continue to cope with. Figures for 2010 show that in England:

> Overall, the main reason why social care services first engaged with children who started to be looked after during the year was because of abuse or neglect (52 per cent). This percentage has increased since 2009.
>
> (DfE 2012b)

Case study

Alicia is 6 years old. She lives in a two-parent family, with a white British father and a black African Caribbean mother, and her 8-year-old brother. She was adopted aged 16 months, and her brother (who has different birth parents) was adopted when he was 2 years old.

Alicia is a bright, usually very happy child. Her parents are clearly very caring and spend a lot of time with both children; they come to parents' meetings; her father comes into the classroom to help with reading once a week; they support Alicia with her own schoolwork and they would like her to get involved with other school activities.

However, Alicia does find some aspects of school life very difficult. She needs a lot of reassurance to try something new, and often just panics and refuses to try. She does not want to try any after school clubs – even choir, although she loves singing in class – and she gets very worried if the usual school routine is disrupted. If there is a class outing, one of her parents always has to come along and she sticks very closely with them all the time. If she is told off, even very mildly, she panics and bursts into tears.

Reflective activity

Why might Alicia find some aspects of school life difficult? Reflecting on the material about life in care, and its impact on children, can you think of some reasons for Alicia's anxiety? It might help to go back to the previous chapter to help answer this question.

Who adopts

Adoption is open to a very wide range of people, the British Association for Adoption and Fostering explains (www.baaf.org.uk). Those wishing to adopt have to be over 21 and there is no upper age limit for those who wish to adopt. What is more important is that those wishing to adopt

> have the physical and mental energy to care for demanding children, and [their] lifestyle suggests they will still have that energy when the child is a teenager, or young adult. Older children are among those children who wait the longest so adoption agencies are keen to hear from people who can give a permanent and loving home to an older child.
>
> (www.baaf.org.uk)

Anyone who wishes to adopt will have a criminal record check. However, this does not necessarily mean that someone with a criminal record will be turned down, unless the criminal record is for 'some offences against children' (ibid.). Those wishing to adopt must also have a medical examination and undertake a training programme to prepare them for being adoptive parents. People from all ethnicities can adopt, as can those with disabilities. 'A single person, or one partner in an unmarried couple – heterosexual, lesbian or gay – can adopt. Since 30 December 2005 unmarried couples in England and Wales can apply to adopt jointly' (ibid.).

Those wishing to adopt need to do so through an adoption agency and when they are accepted 'the agency allocates a social worker, who is responsible for the next stages of the process' (ibid.), after which they will need to go through further checks and provide references. Once the process is fully completed the agency they are working with will try and 'match them with a child' (ibid.).

Reflective activity

Go back to the two lists about adoptees you made earlier in the chapter. Do you want to make any revisions to your list? If so, what has changed your mind about whether they would be considered suitable/unsuitable to adopt?

Adoptive parents are introduced to the child or children they will be adopting only after all this has been gone through. At the point when the adoption is being considered there will be a series of meetings, usually including the foster carers too, between the children and adults involved in the proposed adoption. This is to give all parties a chance to get to know each other before the child or children move into their new family home. After 10 weeks, the parent(s) can apply for an adoption order and, when this has gone through, the child becomes a full member of the new family: they have a new name, and the parents have all the same rights and responsibilities as other parents.

This process, which applies to the whole of the UK, is a lot more stringent than the similar process in some other countries, and people looking at it from the outside do often ask why there are so many checks and clearances, especially since 'other' parents are able to have children without any checks at all. These days, far more is known about the implications of adoption and the difficulties children may experience (see below), however smoothly it has gone; and the reality is that most adopted children's experience will not have been smooth, because they will have been adopted from the care system. However, the checks, clearances and training are all done with the aim of ensuring that adopters know what they will be taking on and that everyone is confident that this match has a good chance of working out.

Contact with birth parents

It is now considered very important to tell children – even those who were adopted as babies – that they were adopted, from as early as possible. This is to avoid the children learning about their adoption from anyone else, or feeling that their adoption is a bad thing. This does mean that their new parents have to manage a quite delicate balance: reassuring their children that they were chosen specially, and that they are loved and accepted, while also trying not to upset them or frighten them by telling them anything disturbing about the reasons why they came into care in the first place. Most children now are also still in some kind of contact with their birth families and/or foster carers, albeit contact that is very carefully managed and mediated.

Contact of this sort 'can be anything from an annual letter from the adoptive family detailing the child's progress and development, to the child meeting members of their birth family in person from time to time' (Adoption UK 2012). Adopted children may have regular contact with members of their birth family's extended family: 'grandparents, aunts or uncles, or any other significant connection to the child's birth family. They may also have contact with former foster carers or with siblings who have been adopted elsewhere' (ibid.). When a child is adopted a contact plan is agreed for the child with the fundamental principle to 'always be what is best for the child' (ibid.) and, if it proves necessary, the plan can be altered.

The three main forms of contact are:
- Letterbox: the adoptive and/or birth family correspond at predetermined intervals, with cards and letters sent through the adoption agency
- Telephone: the child/adopter has telephone contact with the person
- Face to face: the child meets the person, usually accompanied by their adoptive parent and an intermediary from the adoption agency

(ibid.)

Inter-country adoption

Inter-country adoption is not very common in the UK; only a few hundred children are adopted this way every year. It can be the subject of considerable contention in the UK since inter-country adoption, by definition, usually takes children from one ethnic and cultural background and places them in a very different context. However, there are some notable exceptions, such as children who are adopted from India by parents of Indian origin.

Many children who have been adopted into the UK from abroad have no idea who their birth families might be, especially if they were adopted from orphanages. However, as reflected on in our discussion about identity in Chapter 2, most adults who adopt children from outside the UK recognise how important it is to keep their adopted children aware of their birth culture and heritage.

Case study

Helen and her husband Louis, who are both white British, adopted their two sons when the boys were aged 6 and 4.

We decided to adopt some years ago. Our local authority was quite straight with us, telling us that if we were looking for a new baby we might as well leave now, because there simply weren't any available. We said we wanted boys, and were happy to take school-age up to 6 and that we'd take brothers. You have to be realistic about what you can and can't take on but we felt we could do this. We also knew that boys were harder to place, and we wanted to make it clear we were perfectly happy to adopt boys.

The local authority did in fact have a couple of brothers in mind for us, but we were only told about this after we'd been approved for adoption. They'd been in care, on and off, for years. They were put into care by their birth mother, and attempts to settle them with their birth mother failed. They were still in contact with her and seeing her.

From the first conversation after our social worker came round to talk to us about the two boys, we were thrilled. All the information we had was from the foster home. They were 4-and-a-half and 6-and-a-half. At the end of our meeting that night in December, she felt she could show us their pictures – and there was no way we wouldn't fight for them. They had very definite personalities – there was no getting away from that. We both felt that these were going to be our children, and that this was going to work.

The challenges of meeting older children for the first time are different. They have a lot of history, they have a lot of questions – and they've been told 'this is your new mummy and daddy' so you have to be very committed to it, because you cannot change your mind after that. We said they could call us by our first names, but they weren't interested, they called us mummy and daddy from the minute they met us. And that was very disconcerting – we hadn't expected it, and it was quite extraordinary. Right away at our first meeting we went off to have ice cream and go to a playground.

Older children, especially, need a very specific programme for the next 2 weeks of what we'd do and where we'd go. We went to their foster home so that they could show us their territory and their toys. Then the next day we went on our own to the cinema. Some days we'd drive them to nursery, sometimes they'd come to our house for tea. Within days we were putting them to bed at their foster home.

Within a week or two, they spent the night at our house for the first time. And each time they came, they brought a toy. By the second time the little one was in tears by the time he had to leave our house. And by the end of two weeks, they were ready to live with us, although we kept them at their nursery for a term so that they had that continuity.

In some ways the transition was shocking for all of us. We went from no children to full-on parenthood. Bath time, temper tantrums, questions you've never been asked before – all those things we'd never had to do. Our younger son went through about 6 months of 'mourning' for his birth family, with a lot of tears, a lot of questions, and a lot of fantasies. At the same time he was getting more confident, and he was realising that someone could bathe him, cuddle him and sing him to sleep – so he was feeling emotionally attached, but also emotionally torn. There's a lot to work through. It's a lot, for a 4-year-old.

His brother's a different case altogether. Being older, he'd been through a lot more and lived through a lot more. He was a very disruptive, angry little boy. A lot of screaming, shouting, throwing things, and temper tantrums. He has a statement of special educational needs, and one of the issues we've all had to face is that he's had behavioural problems which pre-date his going into care.

We've dealt with a lot of that through just everyday life and determinedly acting in the way we felt parents should. He had to learn that other people in a family matter too. Not just the way we eat dinner or the way we act towards our friends, although it was those things too; but what the basic issue of friends are – he didn't know what a friend was because he'd never been anywhere long enough to make friends. He had a terrible time leaving anywhere, even a café, because he thought he'd never go back again. He simply didn't understand that if you behave properly then of course you'll get invited back, but that you do have to behave properly as well. We started by saying 'you'll be thrown out if you do that' and then realised we needed to say 'no, you will have to go back, you'll have to face everyone again'. We had to change his mindset. It comes through routine; going to football every Saturday, and realising that this is what you do every Saturday, and it's not going to change so you don't need to worry about next Saturday. That makes a child more settled.

We went to see some friends for the day when they'd been with us for 6 months. After the day was over we went back to the B&B

where we were staying and the little one started to cry and said 'is this where we're going to live forever, mummy? I don't like it here'. It had never occurred to us that he wouldn't realise we were just staying for a night. It was just horrible. We'd arranged for him to sleep on the floor in a sleeping bag and we thought it would be an adventure for him, but he cried even more because he used to have to sleep on the floor before he came to us. We'd got the whole thing wrong. We had to hurry back the next day so that he could see that everything was where we'd left it. After that, they get to pack their own bags, they can bring what they want, and just know that everything is where they left it. Until you see just how disrupted their life has been to date, it's hard to fathom. But we all learned, and next time we went away to the beach for a week it was fine.

It's been 4 years now. Today, the younger one has very little memory of anything before us. We're very open about it. They see their birth father twice a year, and have occasional contact with their birth mother. They've got regular contact with other members of their birth family – we're very keen on keeping that. Their grandmother before they were adopted is still their grandmother as much as my mum or Louis's. We've joined their family as much as they have joined ours and I think it's very important to take that on. It is complicated, but I have to handle things carefully with the boys.

Our older son is still settling in, in some ways. He is unsettled, and that's because of what he went through. He's a smart kid who's gone through a lot, and who's seen more than he should, and we talk about that a lot. And like any parents, we worry that we've not got things completely right. But we haven't ever had a moment's regret about adopting them.

Reflective activity

Go back to your initial outline of an adopted child in the earlier reflective activity. Has your picture of who might be adopted changed? What is the biggest difference between your initial idea and your current idea of an adopted child? What things have remained the same?

Loss and attachment

Early years settings and school practitioners need to bear in mind that adopted children have often had to live through far more than other children. Many children feel extremely conflicted about their birth parents, however badly they were treated. Many children in this situation can present with some degree of 'attachment difficulties' because they have had such a range of different carers in their lives (including periods when they had no effective carer) before becoming adopted.

Attachment issues in adoption and foster care

The degree to which children in adoption and foster care will be affected by attachment issues will vary widely. Some children will have a greater degree of resilience than others, and some children may have had some positive parenting experience in the past.

The relationship between the extent of early trauma experienced by the child and the degree of attachment issues is therefore not a simple one, as there can be many influential factors; but it is fair to say the older that the child with a chaotic early life and multiple placements is, the more likely they are to show a greater level of attachment difficulties. However, it is important to remember that even a child relinquished as a baby can display attachment issues, whereas an older child may not.

Recognise the behaviour

Children who have attachment difficulties can express this in a wide range of behaviours and it can sometimes be difficult to recognise that the issue is linked to attachment. These behaviours can be broadly categorised as follows:

- Aggression, oppositional or defiant behaviours (e.g. extreme tantrums, open aggression and defiance, or gratuitous violence)
- Hyperactivity, poor concentration and risk taking
- Lying, stealing and manipulative behaviours
- Compulsive caregiving, compliance and self-reliance (the child looks after him or herself as well as their carer)
- Indiscriminate approaches to adults and children (the child may treat their carer the same as stranger adults, or may appear to show more interest in or affection for unfamiliar adults than their familiar carer)

- Social withdrawal (e.g. rejecting behaviour towards the main carers)
- Sexualised behaviour
- Sleeping problems
- Eating problems
- Wetting and soiling
- Self-harm

Acknowledge the problem

When the child who has joined their family starts displaying behaviour which they have difficulties dealing with, many adopters and foster carers can start doubting themselves and their adequacies as the new carers for their child: 'Does this child really like me? Am I the wrong choice to parent this child? Will I ever feel close to this child?' Often the children will be behaving in a way designed to test the 'staying powers' or commitment of their new carers, who are left wondering whether the child really cares for them.

Another difficulty may be that some children with attachment difficulties may behave in a completely 'normal' and even 'charming' way with everyone but their new adoptive or foster parents, leaving the carers very isolated when no-one outside witnesses the more challenging behaviour of their child. Or they may attach to one carer but reject the other, which can create some difficulties within the relationship. It is important for carers to accept that the feelings of frustration or anger they may feel towards their child when he or she displays behaviours linked to attachment issues are normal.

(Reproduced with kind permission from Be my Parent; www.
bemyparent.org.uk/features/attachment-issues-in-adoption-and-
foster-care,65,AR.html, 'Attachment issues in adoption and
foster care')

Working with adoptive parents

Adoptive parents often need support and reassurance too. They can find themselves in a situation in which they have to parent children who are extremely hard work, without much or any professional backup. Adoptive families do break down under this pressure, and problems at school can be a particular flashpoint. There are no official figures, but Adoption UK 'estimates that as many as one-third of adoptions break down and the British Association for Adoption and Fostering (BAAF) estimates that one in five fall apart even before an adoption order is granted' (www.justiceforfamilies.freeforums.org).

This does not mean that all adoptive parents need special support; however, it does mean that it is important for schools to bear in mind that adoptive parents can face quite specific difficulties.

Adopted children's engagement with the education system

Some children's adoption has gone very smoothly, or apparently smoothly, and there are no particular problems during the early years period. Overall, though, adopted children do not do as well educationally as other children. Many of the issues that adopted children face are similar to those faced by children who have also experienced care without being formally adopted.

The charity Adoption UK's 'Inquiry into the educational outcomes of young people in care/from a care background' discusses how 'All children who are adopted will have experienced some form of loss or trauma through being separated from their birth families' (Adoption UK 2010). Children adopted from care or foster homes may be suffering trauma as a result of their experiences before being taken into care. Similarly, they may also have been moved around many times while in care. 'For many children, this trauma may lead to emotional, behavioural or development difficulties, which may also affect the children's abilities to form secure attachments with their new parents' (ibid.).

Being an adoptive parent is not necessarily the same as being a birth parent and may require the adoptive parent(s) to be aware of specialised parenting skills they may need, besides that of simply wanting to love and care for their child. Similarly, EY settings and schools need to be aware that, although, to all intents, it ought now to be the case that being with a loving adoptive family the child's problems are over, this is often far from the truth.

> The trauma of abuse and neglect has a massive, long-term effect on brain and child development . . . while a child may start with their worst behaviour and improve once they are reassured that their teachers and parents are talking to each other and to the child, equally, s/he may behave very well at school and act out their stresses quite excessively at home.
>
> (ibid.)

The possibly chaotic early lives of adopted children may mean that they are always 'hyper vigilant' (ibid.), particularly in looking for anything that may signal their lives are about to change again. 'Any changes at school, such as a teacher, a classroom or a routine, can be distressing for the child and the parents will need the support and understanding of their child's school' (ibid.). Children may also blame themselves for what has happened in terms of their *losing* their birth family, which in turn may lead to lack of confidence and low-self esteem.

> On a yet more simple level, many subjects within the school curriculum are fraught with difficulty for adopted/fostered children. Classwork on

family trees, family timelines or baby pictures, for instance are obvious areas that cause distress and upset.

(ibid.)

In the classroom

Children who have attachment difficulties may have trouble concentrating in class (because they are very watchful and anxious); they may have behavioural difficulties; and they may refuse to be helped. Alternatively, they may be very anxious to please, because they are so frightened of being rejected. They may have a particular need for firm structures and boundaries and it helps to know how things are at home, including times when children are having contact with their birth parents, particularly if this is difficult for them.

The Post Adoption Central Support agency supported by Clackmannanshire Council outlines the following guidance in helping identify and support children who may be dealing with attachment issues. It states that indicators to look for are:

- poor concentration, especially if a child is constantly looking around for threats;
- talking all the time;
- constantly questioning the teacher, because it feels too dangerous to 'get it wrong';
- ignoring instructions, because they are too anxious to listen;
- panicking because there are too many people in the room;
- trying to create chaos, because they feel so internally chaotic;
- refusal to be helped with new work, because they cannot admit to helplessness;
- lying, stealing and making things up, because it is very hard to tell the difference between fantasy and reality; and
- sulkiness in dealing with 'authority', because they have no framework for doing this.

(adapted from Post Adoption Central Support 2012)

Case study

Imagine you are a reception teacher. One of the children in your class is Zachary, who started school 6 months ago.

Zachary is one of the noisiest children in the class, and frequently loses his temper. There have been occasions when you and the teaching assistant have both had to prevent him physically hurting other children, and he often ends up throwing things across the room. If you tell him that his behaviour is unacceptable, he just shrugs and pretends he hasn't heard. It is very hard to get him to pay attention even when the rest of the class is quite happily getting on with a task or listening to a story.

You have also heard Zachary telling other children about his 'big family' including brothers who are 8 and 10. However, as far as you know he is an only child, and he certainly does not have other siblings at the school. He is finding it very hard to make friends, because other parents are worried that he will 'behave badly' at their house and because he is getting a reputation for telling lies.

His mother is concerned that he is becoming singled out as a 'naughty' boy and asked for a meeting with you last week. She explained to you that she and her partner adopted Zachary last year. He was taken into care aged 2. She does not tell you many details about his birth family, but she does say that his mother was a heroin addict and that Zachary was often left on his own for days. He does have older brothers but they were adopted by a different family and Zachary sees them only at quite carefully controlled intervals.

Think about how this information changes how you feel about Zachary. What changes might you make in:

- The way you tell Zachary if his behaviour has been unacceptable?
- How you deal with his attempts to hurt other children?
- How you ask him to pay attention in class?

Can you think of ways that you might be able to reassure Zachary that nobody is going to leave him again, while at the same time making the boundaries clear for him? You might think about:

- Making Zachary aware that you are listening to him – he does not need to throw a tantrum to be taken seriously.
- Moving him physically to a place in the classroom which is near the wall so that he feels safe.
- Avoiding confrontation or threats as far as possible, so that even if Zachary has to be moved from the room it is a positive ('let's go and see Ms X') rather than reinforcing Zachary's belief that nobody wants him.
- Finding ways to reassure Zachary and letting him communicate without words – through music, drama, or painting.
- Explaining absolutely any change in routine or staffing, including supply teachers when you cannot be there.

- Rethinking any sessions on 'my family' for the moment.
- Distraction strategies to help defuse his tantrums.
- Looking for things that Zachary is good at, and praising those.

As Adoption UK (2010) discuss, if EY settings and schools do not recognise the needs of adopted children and ensure they establish supportive links with the child or children's families the consequences can be a 'population of traumatised children' (Adoption UK 2010), particularly when 'ironically . . . many traumatised looked after children have essential education services withdrawn once an adoption order is granted' (ibid.).

10 Families living in poverty

Gianna Knowles

This chapter explores:

- what it means for a child to live in poverty;
- social mobility and social capital: education, poverty and *life-chances*;
- groups more *at risk* of living in poverty; and
- preventing poor children becoming poor adults, the importance of early years and primary education.

What it means for a child to live in poverty

> Poverty blights the life chances of children from low income families, putting them at higher risk of a range of poor outcomes when compared to their more affluent peers.
>
> (Field 2010, p. 27)

This chapter explores why poverty and underachievement seem to be so persistently linked. In Chapter 2 we briefly mentioned the impact of class on achievement in the UK, and poverty and low income are, historically, also a part of Britain's complex class challenge. We have already explored how, in the UK, tensions between different groups with seemingly different cultural attitudes, beliefs and values can deliberately and unconsciously marginalise other groups and actually undermine the chance to take advantage of the possibilities and opportunities on offer; particularly those opportunities that education can offer. Therefore, in this discussion of poverty and low income, we also need to be mindful that there may be a need to consider more than simply a lack of money as obstacles that prevent children and their families overcoming the barrier that poverty can create with regard to achievement at school and in later life.

From the national and community perspective, historical documents show that 'the poor' and caring for the poor was seen as a community issue as far back as Tudor times. Since then successive monarchs and governments have put in place laws to support the poor and in 1947 Britain saw the beginning of what has come to be known as the 'welfare state' (Knowles 2009). In 1945, at the end of the Second World War, the government turned its attention to rebuilding Britain after the ravages of the previous 5 years. William Beveridge had produced a report in 1942 that, through subsequent legislation, laid the foundations of what we now consider to be the welfare we expect government to provide. For example, as a result of the Beveridge report the National Health Service was established, as was a 'national system of benefits' (Page 2007, p. 2) that would 'provide "social security" so that the population would be protected from the "cradle to the grave"' (ibid.).

The welfare provision introduced in the 1940s included free education, free health care, unemployment benefit and social housing. However, the notion that the community and now the government have a duty to provide for the poor has always been a contentious one, and although the UK now has a well-established welfare system there persists a belief that, when it comes to poverty and being poor, it is possible to distinguish between those who are the 'deserving' poor and those who are the 'undeserving' poor. That is, some through no fault of their own find themselves perhaps homeless and unemployed, whereas others, who choose not to take advantage of the opportunities for education and work available, prefer to 'live off' others.

Reflective activity

In an online article for the BBC, Chris Bowlby writes:

> History suggests that every generation struggles to reconcile support for the poor and unemployed with the reluctance of those paying for help to see it offered too freely.
>
> Relieving poverty has always been about much more than handing out money. Morality always lurks in the background . . . Cabinet minister Jeremy Hunt attracted much attention for suggesting the state shouldn't support large families receiving more in benefit than the average wage.
>
> The Archbishop of Canterbury, meanwhile, warned that people often need welfare 'not because they're wicked or stupid or lazy, but because circumstances have been against them'.
>
> (Bowlby 2011)

Now read this:

> Tesco's reported, in the survey they undertook for the Review in one of their east London stores, on what their staff defined as poverty in modern Britain, and how best the Review could cut the supply routes to adult poverty.

> The staff reported on the changing pattern of stealing. Children were now far less inclined to steal sweets. Instead, the targets were sandwiches, to assuage their hunger, and clean underwear which they also lacked.
>
> (Field 2010, p. 15)

Although politicians and the press may disagree on how best to 'solve' the issue of poverty and the problems that it causes, one area of agreement is that living in poverty causes long-term damage, particularly to children. Research increasingly shows that the early life-chances children have will go on to shape a considerable part of their growing up and subsequent adulthood (Field 2010, p. 16).

In 2010 the then newly elected Conservative–Liberal coalition government published *The Foundation Years: Preventing Poor Children Becoming Poor Adults. The Report of the Independent Review on Poverty and Life Chances* (Field 2010). It discussed how a young person living in poverty at 16 has an increased risk of still living in poverty in their early thirties and possibly beyond. However, why poverty persists in this way is harder to understand. The UK has a welfare system that seeks to provide at least minimum support to families; yet poverty still persists.

That being born into poverty can have such an impact on subsequent life outcomes and, as Maslow would suggest, the possibility of achieving self-actualisation, is complex because it is bound up with other factors. For example, there is a strong persistent and inter-generational correlation between poverty and

> characteristics of disadvantage, such as low parental education, unemployment and poor neighbourhoods, rather than poverty itself. Poverty in adulthood is associated with low education, lack of employment and employment experience and, for women, single parenthood.
>
> (Blanden and Gibbons 2006, p. 1)

Measuring poverty

There are a number of ways of measuring poverty. Generally it is based on the notion of the cost of a range of 'goods' seen as necessary to basic survival. This usually includes food, housing or shelter, possibly heat and clothes. Poverty is usually discussed in terms of absolute poverty and relative poverty. Absolute poverty is a way of comparing poverty globally across countries. The United Nations currently sets the absolute poverty figure as being an income of $1.25 a day (www.unstats.un.org). However, cases of absolute poverty as described in this way are an extreme in the UK. Britain is what is usually described as being an economically *developed* country and is one of the countries that belong to the *Group of 8* or G8. This group comprises the 'world's most industrialised nations' (www.guardian.co.uk); other members of the group are the USA, Canada, Russia and Japan. Poverty still exists in these counties, but is defined in relation to the average and median incomes of the individual countries. Defining poverty in this way is known as relative poverty.

> Relative poverty is where some people's way of life and income is so much worse than the general standard of living in the country or region in which they live that they struggle to live a normal life and to participate in ordinary economic, social and cultural activities.
>
> (EAPN 2009)

Therefore, when poverty is discussed in the UK, it usually refers to the notion of relative poverty, or what is sometimes called low income. In Britain a low-income household is one that is living on below 60 per cent of the median income (www.poverty.org). The most up-to-date figures for determining how many households this applies to relates to 2008/9. In 2008/9, 60 per cent of median income (that is low income) was, per week:

- £119 for a single adult;
- £161 for a lone parent with one child under 14;
- £206 for a couple with no children;
- £288 for a couple with two children under 14 (The New Policy Institute 2010).

These figures also show that in 2008/9 the two-parent, two-children families that fell into the low-income category were those who had £288 income a week left to live on, once they had paid their income tax, council tax, housing costs (whether this was rent or mortgage interest), building insurance and any charges for water. Therefore, the £288 represented the money available for everything else, such as food, clothes, heating, travel and leisure activities, including TV. Figures released by the government in 2011 show that:

- 2.8 million children (22 per cent) were in relative income poverty in 2008/09;
- 2.2 million children (17 per cent) were in both low income and material deprivation in 2008/09;
- 1.6 million children (12 per cent) were in absolute poverty in 2008/09.

> (HM Government 2011)

Other ways of measuring poverty

The Centre for Research in Social Policy (CRSP) at Loughborough University, funded by the Joseph Rowntree Foundation and working in collaboration with the Family Budget Unit at York University (www.minimumincomestandard. org), has developed 'an ongoing programme of research to define what level of income is needed to allow a minimum acceptable standard of living in the UK today' (ibid.). Its research paper *A Minimum Income Standard for the UK in 2011* (Hirsch 2011) looks at what families required in 2011 as a minimum income to cover what might be regarded as the basic necessities or 'goods' to survive in the UK; for example minimum food requirements, housing, heating and clothes. However, this particular research group considers not only what is needed as a minimum to survive in Britain, but also 'what you need in order to have the opportunities and choices necessary to participate in society' (Hirsch 2011, p. 9).

What it means for a child to live in poverty, social mobility and social capital: education, poverty and *life-chances*

We have already explored the notion of social capital in Chapter 1, the notion being that in order to thrive and take full advantage of the opportunities available (through education, for example), it is necessary to be able to access a range of different environments and experiences and to gain a range of life skills. This will be discussed again later in this chapter. Success in Britain, in terms of achieving at school and gaining a well-paid job, is dependent on a range of factors, education being one of them. However, access to the social skills that enable a person to make the most of their education and go on to succeed as a result of it is far more subtle and complex.

In exploring further the notion of social capital, Field (2010) explains how lack of income alone is not the only factor that prevents poor children from becoming poor adults. Field argues that in order to break the inter-generational cycle of poverty we need to find ways that 'ensure that parents from poor families know how best to extend the life opportunities of their children' (Field 2010, p. 16). The opportunities Field is referring to here are 'the advantages that many middle class and rich families take for granted and which a significant number of working class parents achieve', although not achieved by all of those who are on low income (Field 2010, p. 16). The notion of social capital explores how, for complex cultural reasons, certain sectors of society are excluded from the advantages enjoyed by others. This is also discussed (see below) by the research from the Social Exclusion Group (EAPN 2009).

Reflective activity

The term social exclusion is used to emphasise the processes which push people to the edge of society, which limit their access to resources and opportunities, curtail their participation in normal social and cultural life leaving them feeling marginalised, powerless and discriminated against.

(EAPN 2009, p. 2)

Think about some of the ideas that have been explored in this book. One of the themes central to many of our discussions is how EY settings and schools can exclude some families by not recognising the needs of those families. In our discussion on identity in Chapter 2 we also explored how identity gives us a sense of belonging, but if we cannot identify with some others, we may exclude them.

If EY settings and schools have policies and procedures that expect certain things to be in place at home for children, then where they are not, for some children, these children will be excluded from those learning activities.

For example, it is usually regarded as good practice in helping children to learn to read that they read with someone at home. Reflect on what you have read so far; why might many children not have the opportunity to read with someone at home?

Think of children who may be in care or be a refugee child with no one at home who can read English, or perhaps have a family life that is disrupted for other reasons such as illness and bereavement; reading might be very low on the list of the family's priorities.

We know children are more likely to become fluent readers if they have the opportunity to choose books, talk about books and share books with others. How could you provide these opportunities in the EY setting or at school for children who might otherwise be excluded from having access to such activities?

This reflective activity shows how, quite unwittingly, we can exclude children from being able to access learning activities; EAPN (2009) describes such children as being vulnerable. They are vulnerable because 'their personal well-being is put at risk by poverty' (EAPN 2009, p. 2), both in the short term and in the long term. For children the long-term risk occurs because of the cumulative effect of not being able to access all the short-term opportunities they are offered. If they are not able to access all the educational opportunities available, and therefore cannot achieve in their learning in the early years, this will have a knock-on effect into primary school and then into secondary school, up to GCSE level and beyond.

Reflective activities

Vulnerable children may not only be excluded from achieving in their learning because lack of money prevents them from accessing opportunities available to other children; some children, for example children in care and refugee children, may also lack the opportunity to engage in activities because there is no one to support them in accessing the activities they want to engage with, or which might be beneficial for their education.

Think about not only the costs involved in joining in even seemingly straightforward activities, such as going to the cinema, but also, for young children particularly, what makes access to these activities possible. What other activities might a child be interested in doing? Perhaps joining a local football club, playing a musical instrument, doing karate or a form of dance.

Now consider not having the language to access these activities or a parent to make them accessible for you. The issue of children being excluded from undertaking certain activities because of lack of money or lack of support is of further concern in those cases where a child may have a particular gift or talent that goes unrecognised or unused because of lack of access to the facilities to nurture it.

Case study

Josie says:

> There are nine of us living at home. My nan lives with us and two uncles. They have to come and live with us because my nan is too old to look after herself and one uncle lost his job and one got kicked out by my aunt. I share a room with my sister and my step-sister. We have bunk beds and another bed. My brother sleeps in his cot in the room with mum and Ken. My nan has what was the dining room and at night my uncles have the TV room. My mum has a job and so does one of my uncles.
>
> Sometimes there are lots of arguments, about who's taking other people's things and who's cooking tea and who wants to go to bed and who wants to watch TV. It's a bit hard sharing a room as there is not much space to put your stuff, but sometimes nan lets me go in with her.

Jessan says:

It's not so bad at the moment, but last year was really bad. Mum and me left home as mum kept getting hit. We went to this place where we had a room in a house with other people like me and mum. We had to share a kitchen and a bathroom and I know mum was really scared part of the time. I had to change school too. But things did get sorted out and we got a flat, but at the moment the roof leaks in my room, so I stay with mum. But she says it will get sorted out.

The Social Exclusion Group also comments that those affected by poverty

often experience a range of different disadvantages which combine to reinforce each other and trap them in poverty. Poverty limits the opportunity for people to reach their full potential. For instance, children growing up in poverty are more likely to suffer poor health, do less well at school and become the next generation of adults at risk of unemployment and long-term poverty.

(EAPN 2009, p. 6)

Poverty and its impact on health

Alongside the well-documented link between poverty and underachievement, equally well documented is the long-term link between poor health and 'low socio-economic status . . . There are concentrations of people with both shorter life expectancy and greater disability in some of the poorest areas of England' (HM Government 2010, p. 17). The report also states: 'A boy born in Kensington and Chelsea has a life expectancy of over 84 years; for a boy born in Islington, less than 5 miles away, it is around 75 years' (ibid.).

Low income, poverty, class and underachievement

Throughout this book we have referred to the term 'class' as in social class. Class is a complex term to define; however, it is necessary to have some understanding of it to be able to explain the way some social groups operate with regard to one another in the UK. In the UK social class is a way of classifying individuals into one of three groups depending on their income and employment (Table 10.1).

Very quickly we can see how difficult it is to assign people to a class simply on the basis of income and employment. Nurses and police officers are a good example, since increasingly the qualification for undertaking these roles and

Table 10.1 Links between employment and class

Class	Employment
Upper class	The wealthiest members of society. Most often the term is used to describe those who have inherited wealth, power and influence and encompasses the British aristocracy
Middle class	Those in professional occupations, usually only achievable through having a university education or equivalent, for example doctors, lawyers and teachers; although it may now encompass nurses, police officers and some managerial positions. Private home ownership is often another determiner of being middle class
Working class	Those in skilled non-manual employment, for example nurses and police officers and some teaching assistants and nursery workers. Those in skilled manual employment such as some aspects of construction work, plumbers and electricians and hairdressers. Partly skilled workers, such as brick layers and unskilled workers such as shop assistants, farm workers and those who work in bars. Those who are not home owners

the responsibilities that these roles involve has increased over time and therefore they cannot now necessarily be classified as simply skilled non-manual employees. Similarly, with the push for home ownership since the 1980s, which saw the beginning of the sale of council housing to tenants, many who may be classed as working class by nature of their employment are now home owners and therefore possibly middle class.

However, class is not just about income and employment and in many ways the most determining factor when discussing which class someone belongs to is the consideration of the values, attitudes and beliefs they hold. As we have already discussed, Bourdieu (Ali *et al.* 2004) explored the weight certain values, attitudes and beliefs can have in terms of social capital. That is, the more your values, attitudes and beliefs are in line with those of the dominant group in society, the more successful you are likely to be. In this way class also relates to 'constructions of identity . . . class is something beneath your clothes, under your skin, in your reflexes, in your psyche, at the very core of your being' (Ali *et al.* 2004, p. 121).

Discussion of class is important since we can see there is a correlation between low income, poverty and class in strictly financial terms and we have already explored how poverty and low income can impact on achievement. As the government states, children from low income families 'are at particularly high risk of poor attainment and developmental outcomes, which can then feed through to poorer outcomes during and after transition into adulthood' (HM Government 2011, p. 18). Similarly, it reports that the attainment gaps between children from low-income families and those from more affluent families may already be present when a child enters an EY setting or starts school. Once established the attainment gap can be very hard to close and

these attainment gaps often carry over into poor adult outcomes. For example, children on Free School Meals in Year 11 were more likely than those not in receipt of Free School Meals to become NEET (Not in Employment, Education or Training) in the following three years.

(HM Government 2011, p. 17)

Reflective activity

The government recognises that the education system cannot alone tackle wider social inequalities. However, at the moment the system appears to compound these and must be oriented to narrowing attainment gaps (HM Government 2011, p. 44).

However, the government does also say that 'the very best schools, in this country and abroad, have shown that children from deprived backgrounds can succeed and thrive when given the right support' (ibid.).

Among the additional support the government is offering schools to help address this issue is the Pupil Premium, which 'will provide additional funding for the most disadvantaged pupils, including those eligible for Free School Meals' (ibid., p. 45). The money is paid to the school dependent on the number of children in the school having free school meals (FSM). It is up to the school to use the money as it wishes to enable it to 'develop local solutions to support pupils' (ibid.).

What, in your view, might constitute the best support for children from low-income families and be an appropriate way of using the Pupil Premium?

Repeated government statistics also show that one of the groups that persistently underachieve is white working-class children, particularly boys (Gilborne and Mirza 2000; DCSF 2010b; Knowles and Lander 2011). This is explored below.

Reflective activity

- In 2007, 62% of the Year 6 pupils eligible for free school meals achieved the expected level in the national tests in English at the end of Key Stage 2.
- For pupils not eligible for free school meals, the figures were 83%.
- The white boys in this group, the majority of them white British,

did slightly less well in English. 55% of these boys achieved level 4 at the end of Key Stage 2.

(OfSTED 2008, p. 4)

It is clear that the association between poverty and underachievement remains strong and that white British boys from low-income backgrounds continue to make less progress than most other groups.

(OfSTED 2008, p. 4)

In the same report OfSTED (2008, pp. 5–7) lists the following factors as those that are successful in raising the attainment of children in these circumstances. Consider any aspects of good practice on the list you are aware of in the EY settings and schools you know.

- A school ethos that considers the needs of individuals, rather than seeing them as part of the 'free school meal' or 'low-income' group. That is, seeing the children and their potential, not their background.
- Identifying the skills that children had not learnt, for whatever reason, that would help them achieve; for example, organisational and time management skills.
- 'The importance of perseverance; any anti-school subculture "left at the gates".'
- Consistent monitoring of achievement, including setting 'realistic but challenging targets'.
- Listening to children and responding to what they say.
- Adults and support staff 'who are flexible and committed, know the [children] well and are sensitive to any difficulties which might arise in their home'.
- 'A good range of emotional support for [children] to enable them to manage anxieties and develop the skills to express their feelings constructively.'
- Links with local agencies that can provide additional support, including emotional and social support.
- Teachers who take into consideration 'individual interests and preferred ways of learning'.

It can be more straightforward to understand how the relationship between low income, poverty and the economic definition of working class can impact on children's capacity to engage with their education, than the more complex notion of how class, with regard to attitudes, values and beliefs, impacts on working-class underachievement for some children. There is a perception that the children and families from some working-class or low-income groups hold cultural attitudes, values and beliefs that are in direct opposition to those that most schools promote. For example, there is a notion of an anti-swot (Younger *et al.* 2005, p. 151) or laddish (ibid.) culture that pressurises, in this instance, boys to deliberately fail to engage with learning and, whatever their capacity to achieve, to opt out. Younger and colleagues (2005) state that schools need to actively counteract this attitude; they assert: 'schools should treat it as they do racism; there should be no tolerance of it. It is an assault upon equal opportunities and results in misery and underachievement' (ibid., p. 151). Similarly, there can be a belief that education beyond a certain level is an expensive waste of time, particularly for some families in which it is more important to have as many members of the family out at work as possible. In the same way the notion of continuing education to university level, incurring huge debt and not having the guarantee of a professional graduate job at the end of the degree programme is alien to some systems of belief. In discussing such attitudes to education Berg (2010, p. 50) quotes a child's father as saying: 'what you need to do in life is figure out how to work, how to make a decent living, without killing yourself'. It may also be the case that what is taught at school is beyond the frame of reference and experience of some children. In Chapter 1 we discussed how, when it is successful, school can be part of enabling a child to self-actualise and achieve well-being. However, if the school does not connect with the child or with helping the child to build confidence and self-esteem, then it is likely the child will disengage from the process, particularly if the child has found something outside school that they can identify with and find fulfilling.

It is sometimes argued that this underachievement of working-class children is because of the dominance of middle-class attitudes, values and beliefs in schools. Children from families that do not share these attitudes and values not only find it difficult to connect with the way learning is presented to them, but are also marginalised and excluded by teachers who cannot or will not teach in a way that does enable the children to achieve. This denigration of values, attitudes and beliefs other than those held by the middle class is characterised by ridiculing those on low incomes or from the working class through the use of the term 'chav'.

Reflective activity

Why is 'chav' still controversial?

For some it has been a satisfying label to pin on Burberry check-wearing louts. But for others, it is a nasty, coded attack on the working class. ' "This is middle class hatred of the white working class, pure and

simple," wrote Tom Hampsen, [the Fabian] Society's editorial direc-
tor. He also called on the Commission for Equality and Human Rights
to take this kind of class discrimination seriously' (BBC 2010). In the
same article, the journalist Polly Toynbee noted that 'chav is seen as
"acceptable class abuse by people asserting superiority over those
they despise"' (ibid.).

> A belief has grown that the aspirational 'decent' working class has
> become middle class, Jones argues. According to this narrative,
> what is left behind is a 'feckless rump' housed on estates, living off
> benefits or working in low status jobs at supermarkets, hairdressers
> or fast food outlets.
>
> Mocking chavs' perceived bad taste and excess has become a
> popular sport [and is] a coded attack on the poor. 'As inequality has
> widened it's a way of people saying that the people at the bottom
> deserve to be there'.
>
> The word chav 'is deeply offensive' and should no longer be
> permitted as a smokescreen for class hatred. Jones disapproves
> of the word 'toff', but asserts it is far less wounding as it mocks the
> powerful rather than the poor.
>
> (BBC 2010)

Groups more at risk of living in poverty

This chapter has explored how poverty can be inter-generational and why it
seems so hard to break the poverty cycle for some families, particularly where
the link between poverty and educational underachievement is not addressed.
It is also the case that some families are more at risk of living in poverty than
others; for example, families that have a disabled family member and some
children and families from particular cultural and ethnic minorities.

The 2011 report *A New Approach to Child Poverty: Tackling the Causes of
Disadvantage and Transforming Families* states:

- There are around 800,000 children in families with a disabled
  member in relative poverty;
- Children from black and minority ethnic families are almost twice as
  likely to live in relative poverty as children from white families;
- There are 1.1 million children in lone parent families living in relative
  poverty and there are 1.1 million children in large families (those
  with three or more children) living in relative poverty.

(HM Government 2011, p. 17)

With regard to the link between poverty and ethnicity, these figures are supported by Platt (2007, p. 1), who writes:

> There are stark differences in poverty rates according to ethnic group. Risks of poverty are highest for Bangladeshis, Pakistanis and Black Africans, but are also above average for Caribbean, Indian and Chinese people. Muslims face much higher poverty risks than other religious groups.

Preventing poor children becoming poor adults

We have explored how, if education does not make the difference for children from low-income and poor families, it is likely they will, in turn, become poor adults. We have explored how 'the disadvantages and barriers that parents experience are the source of this long-term impact' (HM Government 2011, p. 15). For example: 'for children, experience of life in a workless family is associated with lower educational attainment and reduced aspiration to gain employment themselves' (ibid.). The supportive intervention in the early years and throughout primary education is important in enabling 'children to progress and preventing them from becoming the next generation of disadvantaged parents' (ibid., p. 350).

Reflective activity

The more engaged parents and families are in the education of their children, the more likely their children are to succeed in the education system.

(HM Government 2011, p. 39)

Below is a list of good practice with regard to connecting with and supporting families living in poverty, thereby enabling children from such families to achieve at school. Read through the list and consider any other examples of good practice that you have been part of.

- Evidence shows that children achieve more at school when the home environment supports learning and parents share the same aspirations for their children as schools do.
- Parents want their children to do well at school; however, sometimes they do not understand what the school wants from them. They may not understand the language the school uses; not only if they do not understand English, but also if the terminology the

school uses is unfamiliar: terms such as 'phonics', 'numeracy', 'number lines' and 'guided reading'.

- It may be that, as the government claims, the parents you work with 'would welcome more information and support with raising their children' (HM Government 2011, p. 38).
- Some parents are very keen to support the learning of their children but need help in improving their own literacy and numeracy skills, which in turn 'has a knock-on effect on children's progression as well as improving outcomes for parents themselves' (HM Government 2011, p. 39).

11 Families and bereavement

Gianna Knowles

This chapter explores:

- the incidence of children who are bereaved, having lost a close family member;
- the stages of grief and why it impacts on learning;
- cultural and gender differences in dealing with bereavement;
- when a child dies, including when a child loses a sibling;
- when a child loses a parent;
- supporting children bereaved by a death due to suicide; and
- when a children experiences loss because of family breakdown.

The incidence of children who are bereaved, having lost a close family member

Research by the charity Winston's Wish, an organisation that supports bereaved children and families, estimates that 24,000 children each year experience the death of a close family member. This may be a parent, step-parent, sibling, aunt, uncle or grandparent (www.winstonswish.org.uk). This means it is very likely that those working with children in EYs setting and primary schools will be working with a child who has been bereaved. However, many working in EY settings and schools have had very little or no training to know how children and their families might react to bereavement, or in determining the support the child or family might need to support them in coming to terms with the loss, as well as encouraging the children to engage with their learning.

Death happens in families for many reasons. Sometimes it is as a result of old age or illness and the family may have known for some time that the death was expected. Where the death has been anticipated the family may have had the opportunity to prepare for a life without the family member, and the grieving process may have begun even before the death has occurred. They may also have received support from professional services. Where the death has happened suddenly, through a heart attack or accident, those left behind may have a more complex reaction, since there has been no time to 'say goodbye' and the overriding memory of the deceased may be the last conversation with them (Dyregrov *et al.* 2008; www.winstonswish.org. uk). Perhaps still more traumatically some deaths are as a result of suicide, accidental overdoses of drugs or violence at the hands of another. Children who are refugees or asylum seekers may have witnessed considerable violence, sometimes to their own family members. However, Winston's Wish make the point that, 'for a child, how a person died is usually less important than it is for adults. No means or cause of death is better or worse than another for a grieving child. They are all overwhelming' (www.winstonswish.org.uk).

The following sections of this chapter will explore what might be expected reactions to death in the family and how best EY settings and schools can support children and their families in dealing with the death of a close family member.

The stages of grief

Currently, there is a mixed response to the notion that grief takes the form of marked stages, or that the different characteristics of grief are experienced in a particular order. However, what most theorists do agree on is that there are certain feelings, moods and behaviours that people will experience in the grieving process, although no two people may grieve in the same way. Similarly, theorists discuss how grieving is usually different for or manifests itself differently in adults and children (Dyregrov 2008; Dyregrov *et al.* 2008; Hooyman 2008; Knowles 2011).

Some of the common reactions adults will experience as part of grief are 'a shock phase, which follows directly after the death, a reaction phase that comes when we absorb what has happened, and a reorientation phase' (Dyregrov *et al.* 2008, p. 25), which usually signals the beginning of the time when those grieving will begin to find ways of moving on with their lives. However, even this comment suggests that there is a set of phases which the person grieving is 'passing through', when what may happen is that they will move between seeming to be moving on and having days where they seem again overwhelmed by their loss. There can also be an unhelpful prevailing tendency to believe that those grieving should 'let it out' and that grief should be marked by a noticeable beginning and end.

Case study

Kara says:

> My husband Mark died of cancer 2 years ago. He was 39, he was ill for a year before he died. We have two girls who are now 7 and 9. While he was ill I had a lot of support from my family, both practical

help and financial support. There was also a lot of support from organisations like the Macmillan nurses. When it happened, when he actually died I knew it was coming and I wanted to be strong for the girls and then there was everything to arrange for the funeral. Again my family, especially my mum, were brilliant. Looking back now I can see that I wasn't thinking about me, I wanted to make things OK for Mark and the girls and then there seemed to be so much to do and I had to keep going to keep things together. Now I feel worse than I did when it all happened. The girls are growing up and Mark is not there to ask 'what do we do about this?' I feel lonely and sometimes angry that I am left to deal with this all by myself. I cry now more than I did at first; it's like a realisation of what the future is going to be like now without Mark and without a husband. Mark's family seem to have got through this and his mum, who was in pieces at first, says I must get on with things. I think, I did get on with things, and you were in bits, now I need some comfort and some hope.

As we can see from Kara's account, for many the pressures of day-to-day life may impact on the actual time and space they have for grieving. In such cases the process of grieving, as Kara has realised, has no fixed stages or necessarily an end. For her, grieving for her husband will be a long-term process as it has had such an impact on the future life she had envisaged for herself with her husband and their children. In the same way, and for similar reasons, for many parents grieving over the death of a child is a long-term process, so much so that some will describe it as a way of life. That is, it becomes about 'coping' and is never about forgetting about the person who is now dead.

It is of particular importance to note that grief research has shown how meaningful it is for many to be allowed to develop and maintain an internal memory or a so-called internal representation of the deceased. From being a person inhabiting our external surroundings, the deceased will become a 'person' inhabiting our internal space.

(Dyregrov *et al*. 2008, p. 26)

Common features of grief

As might be expected the features of grief include feelings of shock, possibly disbelief and numbness. Those experiencing grieving may weep, feel intense sadness and yearn for the person who has died.

Immediate reactions, particularly in instances of sudden or unexpected death, include numbness and a sense of disbelief. In some ways this is a coping mechanism to allow the person grieving to begin to process what has happened, while seeking to maintain some sense of 'normal life' for themselves and those around them. The grieving person can then deal with the practicalities of what has happened as well as find a way to begin to come to terms with what has happened.

Guilt may also be a feature of grieving; the person grieving may feel guilty about circumstances surrounding the death or that they 'did not do' something they felt they should have for the person now dead – possibly even say 'goodbye'. Often people will feel guilty if the last time they saw the person alive they argued with them, or felt they never let the deceased know how much they cared about them.

Grief can also be manifest as 'sleep disturbances, anxiety and vulnerability, concentration and memory problems, irritation and anger [and] physical ailments' (Dyregrov *et al.* 2008, p. 29). Anxiety can exhibit itself in concern that something is going to happen to other family members.

For many, 'coming to terms' with the death of the family member after the activity of the funeral involves working through the often intense feelings that will surround day-to-day activities which the deceased was part of. The absence of the lost loved one can be felt as a physical absence, as they are missing from their place at the family table, they are not there to collect the children from swimming, their dirty laundry is still waiting to be washed.

Where the death may have happened in particularly traumatic or tragic circumstances, possibly having been witnessed by the person now grieving, the bereaved may have so-called 'flashbacks . . . Reliving such memories or images can be troublesome and they can reappear in such a way that the bereaved feels that they have no control over them' (Dyregrov *et al.* 2008, p. 31).

Fatigue may also be a symptom of grief, and grieving can use up huge amounts of energy; experiencing and dealing with a complex range of emotions as well as trying to 'keep going' can take its toll, both on energy levels and on the body's immune system. Those experiencing grief may also be susceptible to illnesses.

In some instances the person grieving may seem so overwhelmed by their grief that they seem to begin to fail to function at even the most basic day-to-day level. Such complicated and complex grief reactions will need professional help and support to deal with. It is hard for an onlooker to know when grief takes on this more desperate form.

However, that the person may not seem to be picking up aspects of their life, deny that the deceased has gone and speak of suicide to enable them to 'join' the deceased, may be indications. Many of those who are grieving and are parents of children or young people will make some attempt, however they are feeling, to get on with things for the sake of the children. Early years settings and schools can be the first to notice where the grieving may have taken on this more complex form as they may notice the children becoming seemingly neglected, late for school and/or poorly nourished. In such instances schools need to be aware of who they can contact to seek help for the family (Archer 1999; Dyregrov 2008; Dyregrov *et al.* 2008; Knowles 2011).

Early years settings and schools need to be aware that some of the signs of grief to expect include 'a lack of energy, sleep disturbances, appetite and weight problems, increased emotional and physical restlessness, guilt, social withdrawal, concentration problems and varying degrees of difficulties at school' (Dyregrov *et al.* 2008, p. 71). Early years settings and schools can also be wary sometimes about how they approach discussing terminal illness of a parent or sibling with a child, and similarly discussing funerals and how to remember the person who has died. It may also be the case that some children and families will not be able to cope emotionally and financially after the death of a family member and may need additional help.

Schools also need to look for signs that the child is seeking to support those at home, by deliberately, or through necessity, taking on a large part of the burden of running the home. In particular, they may be taking on the caregiver role for siblings. Where such a situation would seem to persist the school may need to consider seeking help for the family as it may signal that the adults in the family are struggling to cope both practically and emotionally. Children will also see their parent's suffering as being worse than theirs and possibly be over-compensating for that. Children need support to help them deal with their grief and to allow them to live their lives with responsibilities appropriate to their age.

Cultural differences

Expressing grief has a cultural and possibly gender-related dimension. Different cultures have different rituals with regard to funerals and memorial services. Different cultures will also express grief in different ways. We learn how to express and name the different aspects of our grief through learning from those around us. We also learn about grief, and 'what we should do' in a situation where a loved one has died, from films, stories and other sources around us. These learnt cultural responses and differences are not always obvious and can be very subtly different, even within what seem to be families from the same culture. Families too can develop attitudes, values and beliefs about how different life experiences should be dealt with and how emotional experiences, such as those occasioned by death and grief, should be manifest in public. Although some persons and families will show considerable emotion publicly, others may appear to outsiders to be very reserved almost to the point of not seeming to care. However, as Archer (1999) comments: 'this does not mean that grief is not felt at all' (Archer 1999, p. 67); rather it serves to underline that grief is different for different people. Again, an EY setting or school needs to be particularly sensitive to this as a child who comes from a family or cultural background in which grieving is not done publicly may still be experiencing intense feelings and will need particular support to help them deal with their grief.

Gender differences in experiences of grief

Some couples experience a stress on their relationship after the death of a close loved one. This can be particularly so if the death is that of a child. Some of this strain can be put down to factors we have already discussed, namely that individuals express grief in different ways. Therefore, where the different adults in a family are dealing with their grief in different ways tensions can arise between them as they each accuse the other of 'not caring' or 'not understanding'.

Cultural understandings of how men and women ought to behave can also exacerbate the differences in the grieving process. For example, it is very much the norm in many cultures that women are allowed to cry openly whereas men should be strong and silent. This can work against both genders as well as providing them with support. Women who do not wish to cry, or find themselves experiencing grief such that they cannot cry, can be labelled as unfeeling or uncaring. Men, on the other hand, who may feel very weepy can be accused of being weak.

A woman who lives most of her life in the home and managing home-life and the children may find that the home is a constant reminder of the absent loved one. In this way, being at home can mean that the woman grieving may feel she has no relief from her grief. In contrast, having a place of work and a role outside home can serve both as a diversion and as a relief from grief, since it can provide an identity and purpose outside the home and away from any constant reminders of the deceased. Dyregrov notes that:

> coping styles can make communication within the family difficult, resulting in mutual accusations. Nonetheless, it is a myth that many marriages fall apart as a consequence of the death of a child. Most couples grow closer over time, particularly if they manage to show respect for the differences in reaction patterns.

> (Dyregrov *et al.* 2008, p. 41)

When a child dies, including when a child loses a sibling

For a parent, perhaps one of the hardest losses to come to terms with is the death of a child. Losing a child can be traumatic as it is the loss of someone so full of unrealised potential and un-experienced life; it can strike at the heart of how a family understands itself, its purpose and identity. Parents' identity is bound up with being the parents of that child and when the child dies they lose that aspect of themselves; they are no longer, in the physical sense, that child's parents. In many ways they need to reinvent themselves and who they are, without that child. Many parents cannot or do not wish to do this as they see it as being a betrayal of the dead child and something that will negate the whole existence of that terribly important person. For most parents in this situation losing a child is a long-term grief and it cannot be any other way since they will be constantly reminded of the lost child as birthday anniversaries come and go and they see children of the same age and who might have been friends of their child growing up and living their lives. There will always be constant reminders of the child who is not there. Parents in this situation need to be helped to find a way of holding the memory of the child in such a way as to feel reassured that the child is not forgotten and that they are still that child's parents, but in a way that allows them to carry on with their own lives. Parents in this situation may need to talk about their children, and want others who knew the child to talk about them too, even many years after the death has happened. Many parents seek out ways of marking the life of their child, particularly through setting up or supporting charities.

The death of a child can also mean that surviving siblings have been left behind. Children who have lost brothers and sisters can sometimes have their grief masked or overlooked by concern for the parents who have lost their child.

> It is nonetheless young people's daily surroundings that are particularly crucial to the grieving process. Children have the best conditions for coping if they are living with resourceful parents in a stable life situation, if the climate of communication is good and mutual support exists within the family. For older children and young people, support from friends, the school, and other social networks plays an increasingly important role.
>
> (Dyregrov *et al.* 2008, p. 72)

When a child loses a parent

> Among different types of deaths, the death of a parent has the greatest consequences for a child. Not only do they lose a person who is responsible for love and daily care, but the death often leads to less stability and an overturning of their daily life.
>
> (Dyregrov 2008, p. 47)

For most children the most traumatic family death is that of a parent. Dyregrov comments that many children who experience the death of 'close family members will cope well in childhood and adult life' (ibid.); however, the death of a parent may have a much more long-term impact and lead to problems in later life such as depression, alcohol or drug misuse and attachment issues.

Very young children may have little understanding or comprehension of what has happened and experience the loss in ways that seem similar to children exhibiting attachment disorders (see Chapter 5). Very young children may show signs of anxiety or anger, or they may become withdrawn or very clingy to those who are there to provide comfort and security for them. In part, their behaviour will reflect their inability, due to age, to articulate what they are thinking and feeling. As young children grow up and become more aware of what has happened they will want to know about the parent they may feel they never really knew. They may ask many questions about the parent or want to see photographs or video footage, and they will be particularly interested in any evidence, photographs for example, of themselves with the parent. Older children, from the ages of 5 onwards, will begin to have more of an understanding of what has happened, although they will have little life experience or wider contextual understanding to begin to make sense of what has happened. At this age children may have seemingly very confused understandings of what has happened and they may be unable to separate themselves out from what has occurred. For example, children may feel that what has happened is their fault; that the parent died because they had been naughty.

In the initial stages, immediately after the death has occurred, some children may not even cry and may seem very forward-looking and practical; this can be mistaken for the child not caring. In effect, what is happening is that the child's emotional systems are protecting the child from what might otherwise be a debilitating shock and giving them time to begin to come to terms with what has happened. Children may construct explanations for the absence, which adults recognise as being fantasies: stories involving the lost loved one turning up unexpectedly explaining how they had been suffering from memory loss, or were kidnapped, or in hospital and could not contact others, for example. The child will know these are stories but, again, such thoughts are part of their coping mechanism. Similarly, it has long been recognised that in traumatic situations or after painful events children will replay the events though play situations.

Reflective activity

Strategies that can support children in understanding and coming to terms with the death of a close family member

Most advice (Dyregrov 2008; Dyregrov *et al.* 2008; Hooyman 2008; Knowles 2011) agrees that children's questions should be answered as honestly as possible. That is, they should not be misled into thinking that the deceased is simply away somewhere for a prolonged stay, as the child will always be expecting that they will return. Such thoughts also delay the inevitable coming to terms with the truth of what has happened and will delay the grieving process. The child may also feel upset and resentful that they have been allowed to be misled.

However death is explained to the child, it is better that they understand that what has happened is permanent. Children will also often reconfigure what they are told so it makes sense for them. Hooyman (2008) cites the example of a two-and-a-half-year-old, who on hearing of the death of a much-loved neighbour wanted to know about what being dead meant. The parents say that they sought to provide an explanation to the child in terms of their belief system:

> when a person dies, the spirit leaves the body, so without this energy, the body is lifeless. We explained what he would likely see at the funeral, noting that there would be people crying because they would miss Mr. S. and that the body would lie lifeless in a casket at the front of the room for people to visit one last time before it was buried. We explained that the body would be cold to the touch because it no longer had a spirit to keep it warm or keep the blood flowing.
>
> (Hooyman 2008, p. 121)

The parents were concerned that they had maybe not done the right thing or that they had overwhelmed the child with too much information. However, they go on to comment that later they overheard the child explaining 'that Mr. S. was dead and couldn't live in his house anymore because his spirit had left his body. He seemed to understand' (ibid.). Being honest may be very upsetting for the others around the child to have to deal with, since they may not wish the child to see how upset they are. However, it gives the child a better context to understand the situation in if they know that others are upset too; they will see that it is normal and to a certain extent that people are expected to be upset and that they too can be sad.

It is also generally agreed that children benefit from being part of the family's cultural rituals for the funeral of the deceased loved one. It allows the child to be part of the final 'goodbye' and to have some sense of where the person 'has gone'. As stated above, children understand that it is all right to cry and be sad, because others are sad too. And, where death is more timely, perhaps in the case of an older relative such as a grandparent, they can see that, even in sadness, good, happy things about their grandparent are remembered too.

Many families will also find their own ways and rituals for remembering or celebrating the life of their lost loved one, often related to an anniversary such as the loved one's birthday. These can be very supportive for children, as they can be for many family members, because they serve to 'keep alive' the memory of the deceased and provide a vehicle for 'allowing' the person to be spoken about and remembered, and perhaps mementoes, photographs and letters looked at and talked about. Families will often make a 'memory box' containing mementoes of the deceased, in part for this purpose. Where the death was the result of an illness the deceased themselves may have contributed to the 'memory box', wanting to leave letters and videos to help the remaining family after their death.

In many ways it is often the surviving adults who find such rituals and 'memory boxes' more upsetting than children. Adults may feel reminded of things they were beginning to come to terms with, whereas for children they can be very important ways of helping them develop their sense of self. As children grow up their understanding about the death will change and they will need to re-visit what has happened as they begin to re-work their understanding. Significant events in the life of the child may also trigger questions and interest. For example, when a child learns to read they may want to know what their lost parent used to read. As they get older and begin to find themselves as young adults they may want to know what music their parent liked, what clothes they wore, if they liked school, what GCSEs they took. Such questions help the young person identify with the parent, even though the parent is no longer around, and, in many ways, these are just the questions children ask of living parents. As we have seen in Chapter 2 children and young people develop their sense of self, in part, by understanding how they are part of the continuum and wider community of their family and extended family.

In instances of the loss of a parent it is not uncommon for a child's initial coping strategy to be one of denial that the parent is dead. This does not negate what has been said earlier about being honest with the child and allowing them to attend the funeral; it is just that a child can be capable of holding two conflicting ideas and having them make sense in their own mind (Archer 1999; Dyregrov *et al.* 2008; Knowles 2011).

As part of the grieving process children may discuss the parent or lost loved one as if they are still around. Dyregrov (2008) explains how, for the child, this is a strategy used to bridge their own management of grief until they can psychologically move from a situation where the loved one was still present to being able to face the idea of the person being gone forever. Dyregrov discusses how the child may behave as if the loved one is still present in their life, perhaps using fantasy, such as thinking about the loved one as being 'on holiday', until they are ready to deal with the reality. The child may also 'play out' the events of the loved one's death, although in the 'play' version the situation will end happily with the loved one coming back. Dyregrov writes that in such circumstances 'fantasies of reunion are common, and children may express the wish to die themselves so that they may be reunited with their loved one' (Dyregrov 2008, p. 48).

Supporting children bereaved by a death due to suicide

The death of a loved one through suicide can be a particularly difficult loss for all those involved to come to terms with. Although young children may not fully understand the difference between the notion of taking one's own life and death that occurs as a result of other events, older children and adults who do understand may need to deal with additional feelings of guilt and anger, alongside the expected grief emotions. Suicide challenges those left behind since by the very act of having taken their own life the person who has committed suicide is making the statement that they 'had thought life not worth living' (Hooyman 2008, p. 156) and those left behind may feel guilt that they were not able to prevent the event happening. Suicide can also be described as an act of violence: the ultimate act of self-harm and an act of emotional violence towards those left behind.

In the wider social sphere, particularly in cultures that derive from a Judeo-Christian foundation, suicide can be regarded as 'unnatural and carries a social stigma' (Hooyman 2008, p. 157). For these reasons 'it can leave a legacy of shame, regret, reproach, guilt, and damaged self-image for the survivors' (ibid.). The death by suicide of young people is, again, a particularly painful and tragic event for families to deal with and 'suicide is the third leading cause of death among adolescents and young adults, after motor vehicle accidents and homicides' (Hooyman 2008, p. 156). The suicide of a young person can leave the family with very long-term grieving and bereavement emotions to deal with and can have a ripple effect though the young person's local community, particularly amongst their friends and across the school they attended. We have already discussed how children and young people can be vulnerable because their more restricted life experiences provide them with less of a frame of reference to place difficult life events in. That is, they do not yet have the breadth of life experience to understand how things can change and situations do not remain the same forever. For vulnerable young people who may be dealing with identity issues and their own search for identity, 'a peer's death by suicide is especially threatening' (ibid.). The suicide of another young person 'because it is self-inflicted and often violent and taps into the adolescent survivors' fears about the future and capacity to manage' (ibid.), can mean that some young people will pick up the message that suicide *is* the only way to deal with what, at the time, seem to be overwhelming and insurmountable problems.

Dealing with children and young people with suicidal thoughts

Dealing with a child or young person who you suspect, for whatever reasons, may be having suicidal thoughts is again something that you cannot deal with professionally without appropriate training and support.

Check your school's policy for procedure relating to this issue. The policy should inform you of whom in the school to talk to and a list of contact numbers for both the school and the young people to use to address the situation. Check the following sites for help and information:

Calm: www.thecalmzone.net
HopeLine UK: www.papyrus.org.uk
Samaritans: www.samaritans.org
Youth to Youth: www.youth2youth.co

Even seemingly quite young children can be very serious about suicide, particularly if they have heard older siblings or parents talking about it.

Children may be particularly vulnerable after a parent's or sibling's suicide as the now deceased may have shared things with them that they did not tell others:

> siblings rather than parents more commonly will find out about other young people. While very many parents with their background knowledge about the deceased do not understand why the suicide happened, siblings can have had access to other kinds of information, which enables them to know or guess why.
>
> (Dyregrov *et al.* 2008, p. 77)

In such circumstances children may be doubly upset about not having told anyone about how the now deceased was feeling, or they may feel directly responsible for what has happened.

Children experiencing loss because of family breakdown

Although we have discussed aspects of grief as they relate to the death of a close family member, many children will suffer grief and bereavement when they lose contact with family for other reasons. Previous chapters in this book have explored how children may lose contact with their family and family members through family breakdown, through becoming a fostered child or a child in care, through being adopted or through the need to seek asylum. Aspects of grief and bereavement relating to loss may take many forms and may not appear until months or years after what might be seen as the actual event. Children who were quite young at the time they were fostered or adopted, or even when their parents separated and they become members of new step-families, may not begin to mourn the loss of what has gone until they are old enough to understand what they have lost.

For the reasons just listed, it is important to bear in mind that, even when you believe a child seems to have been in a stable family situation for a number of years, learning activities relating to the family may still trigger grief symptoms relating to previous episodes in the child's life. For some children it is not until they begin to understand how their experiences have been different from the experiences of others that they start to realise what has happened to them and start to need to come to terms with what they have lost.

Case study

Chelsea says:

> my parents broke up when I was 2. They quickly married again and had more children with their new partners. My step-mother, Jeanette, also had two children from her previous marriage. From as early as I can remember my life was about staying with my mum or my dad and having lots of brothers and sisters. I remember when I was 8 we were talking about families and I suddenly realised that Jeanette and her children, and my mum's partner weren't related to me, like the other members of my family, and that other people referred to them as 'step-this' and 'step-that'. I remember crying uncontrollably and shouting at the teacher that all these people were my family, not STEP people.

Children who have complex family backgrounds may, when they begin to understand the wider social context their own family fit into, have a reaction similar to the one Chelsea describes. For some children, growing through this time of understanding may occasion the range of symptoms we have explored relating to grief. In coming to terms with their new understandings they will need time and understanding and the opportunity to talk to people who can answer their questions and provide reassurance and support. In many ways they are having to adjust their identity to encompass this newly understood aspect of who they are.

This chapter can only provide guidance about how children may react to being bereaved and how they may deal with loss. It can only offer guidance about such issues as how to 'talk about death' with the child and family and how to support the child in managing their feelings, thoughts and behaviour. Again, training from professionals who deal directly with these issues is the best way of providing children with the necessary support they need.

As with adults, what helps children most to grieve and begin to find a way of moving on with their lives is the support they derive from those around them, including from EY settings and schools. For some children being in the setting or school can provide a relief, as discussed earlier in relation to adults and having a work place to go to. In school nothing has changed and the routines and expectations are a known quantity. Schools need to be particularly aware of this, since children may appear to be as they always have been; however, their 'normal' behaviour may be a coping strategy and does not mean they are not still experiencing considerable unhappiness. Children may derive less support from friends than would be expected for adults in the same situation. This is because other children may not have had the same experiences and, being children, may be unable to relate to the bereaved child's feelings and behaviour. Bereaved children may derive support from other children's friendship only when they can be put in touch with children who have been bereaved too.

Reflective activity

A summary checklist of good practice in supporting bereaved children

Many children will derive comfort from being at school, but may need 'space' at school. For example, schools need to be aware that attendance may be intermittent and they should be sensitive in following up absences.

It can be helpful if the children in the bereaved child's class have been told about the death so that they are aware of the grieving child's situation. Depending on the age of the child's classmates the school may also want to give the children some ideas about how the bereaved child might be on return to school and how they might support them.

It can be helpful and a comfort for many children if they know there is a particular adult they can go to when they want to, sometimes just to be with someone. Similarly, this adult needs to be 'keeping an eye' on the child, even if the child is unaware of it.

All staff need to be informed of what has happened; as Sally says, 'when I went back to school after Christmas a teacher asked me how the funeral had gone and my mother hadn't died yet!'

Children may experience concentration difficulties and their achievement may tail off. Schools need to take a balanced approach between engaging the child in their learning and not over-pressurising them.

The school needs to be aware that the grieving may take different forms and seem to come and go. The grieving process may take weeks or months, or resurface on and off over years, particularly as the child grows up and begins to understand the loss in different ways.

The following web-sites and organisations provide resources, activities, training and ideas for those in EY settings and schools working with children and families that are bereaved:

Winston's wish, the charity for bereaved children: www.winstonswish.
    org.uk
British Heart Foundation: www.bhf.org.uk
Child Bereavement Charity: www.childbereavement.org.uk

Bibliography

Abbott, L. and Langston, A. (2006) *Parents Matter: Supporting the Birth to Three Matters Framework*. Maidenhead, UK: Open University Press.

Adoption UK (2010) 'Inquiry into the Educational Outcomes of Young People in Care/ From a Care Background'. Available online at: www.adoptionuk.org/files/234383/ FileName/Educationoutcomesofyoungpeopleincare-AdoptionUKresponse-13September2010.pdf (accessed 12 February 2012).

Adoption UK (2012) 'Birth Family Contact'. Available online at: www.adoptionuk. org/information/100172/100262/102995/contact/ (accessed 12 February 2012).

Ali, S., Benjamin, S. and Mauthner, M. (eds) (2004) *Politics of Gender and Education*. Gordonsville, VA: Palgrave Macmillan.

Almond, B. (2006) *Fragmenting Family*. Oxford: Oxford University Press.

Archer, C. (ed.) (2003) *Trauma, Attachment, and Family Permanence: Fear Can Stop You Loving*. London: Jessica Kingsley Publishers.

Archer, J. (1999) *Nature of Grief: The Evolution and Psychology of Reactions to Loss*. Florence, KY: Brunner-Routledge.

Arnaut, G. L. Y., Fromme, D. K., Stoll, B. M. and Felker, J. A. (2000) 'A Qualitative Analysis of Stepfamilies: The Biological Parent'. *Journal of Divorce & Remarriage*, 33(3/4): 111–128.

Barn, R. and Harman, V. (2012) 'Do Racist Attitudes Hinder Mothers of Mixed-Race Children?' Available online at: www.rhul.ac.uk/aboutus/newsandevents/news/ newsarticles/doracistattitudeshindermothersofmixed-racechildren.aspx (accessed 13 February 2012).

Barnard, A. (2000) *History and Theory in Anthropology*. Port Chester, NY: Cambridge University Press.

BBC (2010) 'Why Is 'Chav' Still Controversial?' Available online at: www.bbc.co.uk/ news/magazine-13626046 (accessed 16 February 2012).

BBC (2012a) 'Windrush: Arrivals'. Available online at: www.bbc.co.uk/history/brit-ish/modern/arrival_01.shtml (accessed 5 February 2012).

BBC (2012b) 'WW2 People's War'. Available online at: www.bbc.co.uk/ww2peo-pleswar/timeline/factfiles/nonflash/a6651218.shtml (accessed 5 February 2012).

Beller, S. (2007) *Antisemitism: A Very Short Introduction*. Oxford, UK: Oxford University Press.

Bennett, E. (2009) 'What Makes My Family Stronger: A Report into What Makes Families with Disabled Children Stronger – Socially, Emotionally and Practically'. London: Contact A Family. Available online at: www.cafamily.org.uk/pdfs/wmmfs. pdf (accessed 21 June 2011).

Berg, G. (2010) *Low-Income Students and the Perpetuation of Inequality: Higher Education in America Farnham*. Farnham, UK: Ashgate Publishing Group.

Bernardes, J. (1997) *Family Studies: An Introduction*. London: Routledge.

Blanden, J. and Gibbons, S. (2006) *The Persistence of Poverty across Generations: A View from Two British Cohorts for the Joseph Rowntree Foundation by The Policy Press*. York, UK: Joseph Rowntree Foundation.

Bowlby, C. (2011) 'The Deserving or Undeserving Poor?' Available online at: www. bbc.co.uk/news/magazine-11778284 (accessed 19 August 2011).

Brannen, J., Heptinstall, E. and Bhopal, D. (2000) *Connecting Children: Core and Family Life in Later Childhood*. Florence, KY: Routledge.

British Association for Adoption and Fostering (2012) 'All about Fostering'. Available online at: www.baaf.org.uk/info/fostering (accessed 14 February 2012).

British Refugee Council (2012) 'Tell It Like It Is: The Truth about Asylum'. British Refugee Council. Available online at: www.refugeecouncil.org.uk/practice/basics/ facts.htm?WBCMODE='#factfive (accessed 5 February 2012).

Burr, V. (1998) *Gender and Social Psychology*. London: Routledge.

Caballero, C. and Edwards, R. (2010) *Lone Mothers of Mixed Racial and Ethnic Children: Then and Now*. London: Runnymede.

Caballero, C., Edwards, R. and Puthussery, S. (2008) *Parenting 'Mixed' Children: Negotiating Difference and Belonging in Mixed Race, Ethnicity and Faith Families*. London: Joseph Rowntree Foundation.

Caron, V. (1998) *Uneasy Asylum: France and the Jewish Refugee Crisis, 1933–1942*. Stanford, CA: Stanford University Press.

Carter, P. (2005) *Keepin' It Real: School Success beyond Black and White*. Cary, NC: Oxford University Press.

Chambers, D. (2001) *Representing the Family*. London: Sage Publications.

Charter of the United Nations (2012) 'Preamble'. Available online at: www.un.org/ en/documents/charter/preamble.shtml (accessed 18 February 2012).

Clarkson, J., Frank, J., Lucantoni, L. and Fox, A. (2008) 'Emotional Support for Young Carers: A Report Prepared for the Royal College of Psychiatrists by The Children's Society Young Carers Initiative and The Princess Royal Trust for Carers'. Available online at: www.rcpsych.ac.uk/mentalhealthinfoforall/youngpeople/ caringforyoungcarers/emotionalsupport.aspx (accessed 21 June 2011).

Cleaver, H. (2000) 'Fostering Family Contact: A Study of Children, Parents and Foster Carers'. London: The Stationery Office.

Coello, L. (2010) *Significant Difference?: A Comparative Analysis of Multicultural Policies in the United Kingdom and the Netherlands*. Amsterdam: Amsterdam University Press.

Cooper, P. (2007) *Nurture Groups in School and at Home: Connecting with Children with Social, Emotional and Behavioural Difficulties*. London: Jessica Kingsley Publishers.

Covey, H. (2010) *Street Gangs throughout the World* (2nd edn). Springfield, IL: Charles C. Thomas.

Cramb, A. (2009) 'Mother's Anger over Gay Couple's Adoption of her Children'. Available online at: www.telegraph.co.uk/news/uknews/scotland/4379200/ Mothers-anger-over-gay-couples-adoption-of-her-children.html (accessed 1 May 2012).

Daily Mail (2012) 'Santorum Booed for Suggesting Gay Marriage "Harms" Children as He Defends 2003 Interview Linking Homosexuality to "Man on Dog" Sex'. Available online at: www.dailymail.co.uk/news/article-2082981/

Rick-Santorum-booed-suggesting-gay-marriage-harms-children.html (accessed 8 January 2012).

Danziger, S. H. (ed.) (2001) *Understanding Poverty*. Cambridge, MA: Harvard University Press.

Davies, C. (2011) 'Adoption System Changes Planned to Speed Up Process'. *The Guardian*, 22 December. Available online at: www.guardian.co.uk/society/2011/dec/22/adoption-system-changes (accessed 8 January 2012).

DCSF (Department for Children, Schools and Families) (2009a) 'Improving the Educational Attainment of Children in Care (Looked After Children)'. Available online at: www.teachernet.gov.uk/publications (accessed 8 May 2012).

DCSF (2009b) *Gender Issues in School: What Works to Improve Achievement for Boys and Girls*. Nottingham: DCSF Publications.

DCSF (2010a) *Support for All: The Families and Relationships Green Paper*. Norwich: The Stationery Office.

DCSF (2010b) 'Making an Impact on Black Children's Achievement: Examples of Good Practice from the Black Children's Achievement Programme'. Available online at: http://dera.ioe.ac.uk/2383/1/ntg_bca_impact_0002210.pdf (accessed 4 May 2012).

DCSF (2010c) 'Outcome Indicators for Children Looked After: Twelve Months to 30 September 2009, England'. Available online at: www.education.gov.uk/rsgateway/DB/SFR/s000930/sfr08–2010.pdf (accessed 14 February 2012).

Dearden, C. and Becker, S. (2004) 'Young Carers in the UK: The 2004 Report'. London: Carers UK. Available online at: www.direct.gov.uk/en/DisabledPeople/Disabledparents/DG_10037906>> (accessed 21 June 2011).

Deater-Deckard, K. (2004) *Parenting Stress*. New Haven, CT: Yale University Press.

Delgado, R. and Stefancic, J. (2001) *Critical Race Theory: An Introduction*. New York: NYU Press.

Department for Education (DfE) (2010) 'Parental Opinion Survey 2010'. Available online at: www.education.gov.uk/publications/eOrderingDownload/DFE-RR061.pdf (accessed 2 May 2012).

Dever, C. (1998) *Death and the Mother from Dickens to Freud: Victorian Fiction and the Anxiety of Origins*. Edinburgh: Oxford University Press.

DfE (2011) 'Teachers' Standards'. Available online at: http://media.education.gov.uk/assets/files/pdf/t/teachers%20standards%20from%20september%202012.pdf (accessed 4 May 2012).

DfE (2012a) 'Refugees, New Arrivals and Asylum Seekers'. Available online at: www.education.gov.uk/a0076728/refugees-new-arrivals-and-asylum-seekers (accessed 4 February 2012).

DfE (2012b) 'Children Looked After by Local Authorities in England (Including Adoption and Care Leavers) – Year Ending 31 March 2010'. Available online at: www.education.gov.uk/rsgateway/DB/SFR/s000960/index.shtml (accessed 12 January 2012).

DfES (2004) *Aiming High: Guidance on Supporting the Education of Asylum Seeking and Refugee Children*. Nottingham: DfES.

DfES (2007) 'Raising the Attainment of Pakistani, Bangladeshi, Somali and Turkish Heritage Pupils'. Available online at: http://dera.ioe.ac.uk/7186/1/62e3813339e65c63dd42387906aef5ef.pdf (accessed 17 May 2012).

Douglas, A. (2011) 'No One Has a Right to Adopt'. *The Guardian*. Available online at: www.guardian.co.uk/commentisfree/2011/dec/22/no-one-has-a-right-to-adopt (accessed 8 January 2012).

Dyregrov, A. (2008) *Grief in Children: A Handbook for Adults*. London: Jessica Kingsley Publishers.

Dyregrov, K., Dyregrov, A. and Raundalen, M. (2008) *Effective Grief and Bereavement Support: The Role of Family, Friends, Colleagues, Schools and Support Professionals*. London: Jessica Kingsley Publishers.

EAPN (European Anti-Poverty Network) Social Inclusion Working Group with the collaboration of Hugh Frazer (2009) 'Poverty and Inequality in the EU'. European Anti Poverty Network: Brussels. Available online at: www.jrf.org.uk/sites/files/jrf/EAPN-explainer.pdf (accessed 8 May 2012).

Edwards. R. (2002) 'Creating Stability for Children in Step-families'. *Children & Society*, 16: 154–167.

Empson, J. (2004) *Atypical Child Development in Context*. London: Palgrave Macmillan.

Fausto-Sterling, A. (2000) *Sexing the Body: Gender Politics and the Construction of Sexuality*. New York: Basic Books.

Field, F. (2010) *The Foundation Years: Preventing Poor Children Becoming Poor Adults. The Report of the Independent Review on Poverty and Life Chances*. London: Cabinet Office.

Fine, B. (2010) *Theories of Social Capital: Researchers Behaving Badly*. London: Pluto Press.

Foley, P., Roche, J. and Tucker, S. (2001) *Children in Society: Contemporary Theory, Policy and Practice*. Basingstoke, UK: Palgrave Macmillan.

Foster, S. (2008) *Human Rights and Civil Liberties* (2nd edn). Dorset, UK: Pearson Education.

Frost, G. (2008) *Living in Sin: Cohabiting as Husband and Wife in Nineteenth-Century England*. Manchester: Manchester University Press.

Garralda, M. E. (2010) *Increasing Awareness of Child and Adolescent Mental Health*. Blue Ridge Summit, PA: Rowman & Littlefield.

Garrett, B. (1998) *Personal Identity and Self-Consciousness*. London: Routledge.

Gilborne, D. and Mirza, H. (2000) *Educational Inequality: Mapping Race, Class and Gender. A Synthesis of Research Evidence*. London: OfSTED.

Gove, M. (2011) 'The Moral Purpose of School Reform'. Available online at: www.education.gov.uk/inthenews/speeches/a0077859/the-moral-purpose-of-school-reform (accessed 8 February 2012).

Grenfell, M. (1998) *Bourdieu and Education: Acts of Practical Theory*. Florence, KY: Taylor & Francis.

Grenfell, M. (ed.) (2008) *Pierre Bourdieu: Key Concepts*. Durham, UK: Acumen.

Grimston J. (2007) 'Mixed-Race Britons to Become Biggest Minority'. *The Sunday Times*, 4 March 2007. Available online at: www.thetimes.co.uk/tto/public/site-search (accessed 12 February 2012).

Guasp, A. (2010) 'Different Families: The Experiences of Children with Lesbian and Gay Parents'. University of Cambridge: Stonewall Education for All. Available online at: www.stonewall.org.uk/what_we_do/2583.asp (accessed 5 May 2012).

Hayman, S. (2001) *Relate Guide to Step Families: Living Successfully with Other People's Children* (Relate Guides). London: Vermillion.

Herbert, J. (2008) *Negotiating Boundaries in the City: Migration Ethnicity Gender in Britain*. Abingdon, Oxon: Ashgate Publishing Group.

Hirsch, D. (2011) *A Minimum Income Standard for the UK in 2011*. York, UK: Joseph Rowntree Foundation.

HM Government (2010) *Child Poverty Act 2010*. London, UK: The Stationery Office.

HM Government (2011) *A New Approach to Child Poverty: Tackling the Causes of Disadvantage and Transforming Families' Lives*. Norwich: The Stationery Office.

Home Office UK Border Agency (2012) 'Visiting the UK'. Available online at: www.ukba.homeoffice.gov.uk/visas-immigration/visiting/ (accessed 4 February 2012).

Hooyman, N. R. (2008) *Living through Loss: Interventions across the Life Span*. New York: Columbia University Press.

Joint Committee on Human Rights (2007) '73 Memorandum from UNHCR'. Available online at: www.publications.parliament.uk/pa/jt200607/jtselect/jtrights/81/81we83.htm (accessed 5 February 2012).

Kennedy, S. (2010) 'Child Poverty Act 2010: A Short Guide'. Available online at: www.parliament.uk/briefingpapers/commons/lib/research/briefings/snsp-05585.pdf (accessed 21 May 2011).

Kestenberg, J. and Kahn, C. (eds) (1998) *Children Surviving Persecution: An International Study of Trauma and Healing*. Westport, CT: Greenwood Press.

Kielhorn, J. (2006) *World Health Organization Environmental Health Criteria Series, Number 235: Dermal Absorption*. Geneva, CHE: World Health Organization.

Knowles, C. (2004) *Race and Social Analysis*. London: Sage.

Knowles, G. (2009) *Ensuring Every Child Matters*. Chippenham, UK: Sage.

Knowles, G. (2011) *Supporting Inclusive Practice* (2nd edn). Abingdon: Routledge.

Knowles, G. and Lander, V. (2011) *Diversity, Equality and Achievement in Education*. Chippenham, UK: Sage.

Lawler, S. (2009) *Identity Sociological Perspectives*. Cambridge, UK: Polity Press.

Lee, J.-A. (2005) *Situating Race and Racisms in Time, Space, and Theory: Critical Essays for Activists and Scholars*. Montreal, QC: McGill-Queen's University Press.

Litosseliti, L. and Sunderland, J. (eds) (2002) *Gender Identity and Discourse Analysis*. Philadelphia, PA: John Benjamins Publishing Company.

Loudon, I. (1992) *Death in Childbirth: An International Study of Maternal Care and Maternal Mortality 1800–1950*. Oxford: Clarendon Press.

McKenzie, K. (ed.) (2006) *Social Capital and Mental Health*. London: Jessica Kingsley Publishers.

Mai Sims, J. (ed.) (2007) 'Mixed Heritage: Identity, Policy and Practice'. London: Runnymede. Available online at: www.mix-d.org/about/our-definition (accessed 28 August 2011).

Malesevic, S. (2004) *Sociology of Ethnicity*. London: Sage.

Malloch, T. R., Massey, S. T. and Billington, J. (2006) *Renewing American Culture: The Pursuit of Happiness*. Salem, MA: Scrivener Publishing.

May, T. (2006) *Philosophy of Foucault*. Durham, UK: Acumen.

Mayseless, O. (2002) *Parenting Representations: Theory, Research, and Clinical Implications*. Cambridge, UK: Cambridge University Press.

Mental Health Foundation (2010) 'MyCare: The Challenges Facing Young Carers of Parents with a Severe Mental Illness'. Available online at: www.mentalhealth.org.uk/our-work/research/completed-projects/mycare/ (accessed 8 May 2012).

Mills, S. (2004) *Discourse*. London: Routledge.

Morris, J. and Wates, M. (2006) 'Supporting Disabled Parents and Parents with Additional Support Needs'. Bristol: Social Care Institute for Excellence. Available online at: www.scie.org.uk/publications/knowledgereviews/kr11.pdf (accessed 9 May 2012).

Moses, D. N. (2009) *Promise of Progress: The Life and Work of Lewis Henry Morgan*. Columbia: University of Missouri Press.

Mulholland, H. (2011) 'Duncan Smith Blames Riots on Family Breakdown and Benefits System'. *The Guardian*, 3 October. Available online at: www.guardian. co.uk/politics/2011/oct/03/duncan-smith-riots-benefits-system (accessed 29 December 2011).

New Policy Institute (2010) *Monitoring Poverty and Social Exclusion 2010: Findings Informing Change*. York, UK: Joseph Rowntree Foundation.

Niro, B. (2003) *Race*. Gordonsville, VA: Palgrave Macmillan.

ODPM (Office of the Deputy Prime Minister) (2004) 'Mental Health and Social Exclusion'. Social Exclusion Unit Report. London: ODPM. Available online at: http://www.socialinclusion.org.uk/publications/SEU.pdf (accessed 8 May 2012).

Office for National Statistics (2011) 'Ethnic Breakdown, 2009'. Available online at: https://docs.google.com/spreadsheet/ccc?key=0AonYZs4MzlZbdFJ6OVF1U3JZ TXEyYnFjb0k1clJvOFE&hl=en#gid=0 (accessed 4 May 2012).

Office for National Statistics (2012) 'Historic Adoption Tables'. Available online at: www.ons.gov.uk/ons/publications/re-reference-tables.html?edition=tcm% 3A77–225046 (accessed 12 February 2012).

Office for National Statistics and ESDS (Economic and Social Data Service) Government (2010) 'Ethnicity: Introductory User Guide'. Available online at: www.esds.ac.uk/government/docs/ethnicityintro.pdf (accessed 6 May 2012).

OfSTED (2003) 'Boys' Achievement in Secondary Schools' (HMI 1659). OfSTED Publications Centre. Available online at: www.ofsted.gov.uk/resources/boys-achievement-secondary-schools (accessed 9 May 2012).

OfSTED (2004) 'Promoting and Evaluating Pupils' Spiritual, Moral, Social and Cultural Development'. Available online at: www.ofsted.gov.uk/resources/ promoting-and-evaluating-pupils-spiritual-moral-social-and-cultural-development (accessed 4 May 2012).

OfSTED (2007) 'The Foundation Stage' (HMI 2610). Ofsted Publications Centre. Available online at: www.ofsted.gov.uk/resources/foundation-stage (accessed 9 May 2012).

OfSTED (2008) *White Boys from Low-Income Backgrounds: Good Practice in Schools*. London: OfSTED.

OfSTED (2009) *Care and Prejudice*. London: OfSTED.

OfSTED (2011) 'Girls' Career Aspirations' (No. 090239). OfSTED Publications Centre. Available online at: www.education.gov.uk/publications/eOrderingDownload/090239.pdf (accessed 9 May 2012).

Oldfield, N. and Bradshaw, J. (2011) 'The Costs of a Child in a Low-Income Household'. *Journal of Poverty and Social Justice*, 19(2): 131–143.

Page, R. M. (2007) *Revisiting the Welfare State*. Buckingham, UK: Open University Press.

Pearce, C. (2009) *Short Introduction to Attachment and Attachment Disorder*. London: Jessica Kingsley Publishers.

Pearce, J. (2010) *Adoption UK Response to Inquiry into the Educational Outcomes of Young People in Care/From a Care Background*. Banbury: Adoption UK.

Phillips, M. (2011) 'It's Not Just Absent Fathers, Mr Cameron. Family Breakdown is Driven by Single Mothers on Benefits'. *Daily Mail*, 20 June. Available online at: www.dailymail.co.uk/debate/article-2005677/Family-breakdown-driven-single-mothers-benefits-absent-fathers.html (accessed 30 December 2011).

Platt, L. (2007) *Poverty and Ethnicity in the UK*. York, UK: Joseph Rowntree Foundation.

Platt, L. (2009) 'Ethnicity and Family – Relationships within and between Ethnic Groups: An Analysis Using the Labour Force Survey'. London: Equality and Human Rights Commission. Available online at: www.pre-school.org.uk/practitioners/inclusion/544/how-can-we-support-the-identities-of-our-mixed-heritage-children (accessed 30 August 2011).

Plaza, D. E. and Henry, F. (eds) (2006) *Returning to the Source: The Final Stage of the Caribbean Migration Circuit*. Kingston, Jamaica: UWI Press.

politics.co.uk (2012) 'Immigration Removal/Detention Centres'. Available online at: www.politics.co.uk/reference/immigration-removal-detention-centres (accessed 18 February 2012).

Post Adoption Central Support (2012) 'Adoption, Attachment Issues and Your School'. Available online at: www.postadoptioncentralsupport.org/leaflet.pdf (accessed 12 February 2012).

Prior, V. (2006) *Understanding Attachment and Attachment Disorders: Theory, Evidence and Practice*. London: Jessica Kingsley Publishers.

Rai, R. and Panna, K. (2010) *Introduction to Culture Studies*. Mumbai, India: Global Media.

Raicar, A. M. (2009) *United Kingdom Council for Psychotherapy: Child-Centred Attachment Therapy: The CcAT Programme*. London: Karnac Books.

Rainsford, S. (2011) 'Migrants Pushed towards Exit by Spanish Jobs Crisis'. Available online at: www.bbc.co.uk/news/world-europe-13271505 (accessed 5 February 2012).

Reed-Danahay, D. (2005) *Locating Bourdieu*. Bloomington: Indiana University Press.

Refugee Council (n.d.) 'The Facts about Asylum'. Available online at: www.refugee-council.org.uk/practice/basics/facts.htm?WBCMODE='#factsix (accessed 9 May 2012).

Reid, S. (2009) 'Family in 11th-hour Legal Battle to Halt Brothers' Adoption by Gay Couple'. Available online at: www.dailymail.co.uk/news/article-1167209/Family-11th-hour-legal-battle-halt-brothers-adoption-gay-couple.html (accessed 12 February 2012).

Rennison, N. (2001) *Sigmund Freud*. Harpenden, UK: Pocket Essentials.

Riger, S. (2000) *Transforming Psychology: Gender in Theory and Practice*. Cary, NC: Oxford University Press.

Rivers, I., Poteat, V. P. and Noret, N. (2008) 'Victimization, Social Support, and Psychosocial Functioning among Children of Same-Sex and Opposite-Sex Couples in the United Kingdom'. *Developmental Psychology*, 44(1): 127–134.

Robinson, A. M. (2007) *Multiculturalism and the Foundations of Meaningful Life: Reconciling Autonomy, Identity, and Community*. Vancouver, BC: UBC Press.

Robinson, M. (1993) *Family Transformation during Divorce and Remarriage: A Systematic Approach*. Florence, KY: Routledge.

Rodriguez, R. E. (2005) *Brown Gumshoes: Detective Fiction and the Search for Chicana/o Identity*. Austin: University of Texas Press.

Rogers, S. (2011) 'The Ethnic Population of England and Wales Broken Down by Local Authority'. *The Guardian* Data Blog, 18 May. Available online at: www.guardian.co.uk/news/datablog/2011/may/18/ethnic-population-england-wales#data (accessed 4 May 2012).

Rogers, S. (2012) 'Immigration to the UK: The Key Facts'. *The Guardian* Data Blog, 23 February. Available online at: www.guardian.co.uk/news/datablog/2010/jun/26/non-eu-immigration-uk-statistics (accessed 5 February 2012).

Rosenthal, J. H. and Barry, C. (eds) (2009) *Ethics and International Affairs: A Reader* (3rd edn). Baltimore, MD: Georgetown University Press.

Royal College of Psychiatrists (2004) 'Parents with a Mental Illness: The Problems for Children. Factsheet for Parents and Teachers'. Available online at: www.rcpsych. ac.uk/pdf/Sheet16.pdf (accessed 12 February 2012).

Royal College of Psychiatrists (2009) 'Parental Mental Illness: The Problems for Children. Information for Parents, Carers and Anyone who Works with Young People'. Available online at: www.rcpsych.ac.uk/mentalhealthinfo/mental-healthandgrowingup/parentalmentalillness.aspx (accessed 20 June 2011).

Royal College of Psychiatrists (2012) 'Difficulties for Children'. Available online at: www.rcpsych.ac.uk/mentalhealthinfo/mentalhealthandgrowingup/parentalmen-talillness.aspx (accessed 12 February 2012).

Sarat, A. and Kearns, T. R. (eds) (2001) *Cultural Pluralism, Identity Politics, and the Law*. Ann Arbor, MI: University of Michigan Press.

Schwab, J. J., Gray-Ice, H. M. and Prentice, F. R. (2000) *Family Functioning: The General Living Systems Research Model*. Hingham, MA: Kluwer Academic Publishers.

Selwyn, J., Sturgess, W., Quinton, D. and Baxter, C. (2003) *Costs and Outcomes of Non-Infant Adoptions: Report to the Department for Education and Skills*. London: DFES.

Sexton, J. (2008) *Amalgamation Schemes: Antiblackness and the Critique of Multiracialism*. Minneapolis: University of Minnesota Press.

Sinclair, I. (2005) *Fostering Now: Messages from Research*. London: Jessica Kingsley.

Sinclair, I., Wilson, K. and Gibbs, I. (2004) *Foster Placements: Why They Succeed and Why They Fail*. London: Jessica Kingsley Publishers.

Singh, R. and Sumita, D. (2010) *'Race' and Culture: Tools, Techniques and Trainings: A Manual for Professionals*. London: Karnac Books.

Skuse, T. and Ward, H. (2003) *Listening to Children's Views of Care and Accommodation*. London: Jessica Kingsley Publishers.

Smart, C. (1999) 'Divorce in England 1950–2000: A Moral Tale', CAVA Workshop Paper 2. Prepared for Workshop One: Frameworks for Understanding Policy Change and Culture, Friday 29 October. Available online at: www.leeds.ac.uk/ cava/papers/wsp2.pdf (accessed 10 August 2011).

Smith, L. (2006) 'Absent Voices'. *The Guardian*, 6 September. Available online at: www.guardian.co.uk/society/2006/sep/06/guardiansocietysupplement1 (accessed 30 August 2011).

Social Care Institute for Excellence (2009) 'Think Child, Think Parent, Think Family: A Guide to Parental Mental Health and Child Welfare'. London, SCIE. Available online at: www.scie.org.uk/publications/guides/guide30/index.asp (accessed 20 June 2011).

Spohrer, K. (2008) *Teaching Assistant's Guide to Emotional and Behavioural Difficulties*. London: Continuum International Publishing.

Tasker, F. (2005) 'Lesbian Mothers, Gay Fathers, and Their Children: A Review'. *Journal of Developmental & Behavioral Pediatrics*, 26(3): 224–240. Available online at: http://journals.lww.com/jrnldbp/Abstract/2005/06000/Lesbian_Mothers,_ Gay_Fathers,_and_Their_Children_.12.aspx (accessed 1 November 2011).

TES (2012) 'Second Language, First-Class Results'. Available online at: www.tes. co.uk/article.aspx?storycode=6179208 (accessed 18 February 2012).

The Who Cares? Trust (2010) 'Who Cares . . . about Looked-After Children's Education? A Guide for Foster Carers'. Available online at: www.thewhocarestrust.org.uk/publications.php/41/who-cares...-about-looked-after-childrens-education-a-guide-for-foster-carers (accessed 14 February 2012).

The Who Cares? Trust (2012) 'Supportive Teachers'. Available online at: www.thewhocarestrust.org.uk/pages/supportive-teachers.html (accessed 14 February 2012).

Thoburn, J., Norford, L. and Rashid, S. P. (2000) *Permanent Family Placement for Children of Minority Ethnic Origin*. London: Jessica Kingsley.

Thoburn, J., Chand, A. and Procter, J. (2005) *Child Welfare Services for Minority Ethnic Families: The Research Reviewed*. London: Jessica Kingsley Publishers.

Timms, J. E., Bailey, S. and Thoburn, J. (2007) *Your Shout Too! A Survey of the Views of Children and Young People Involved in Court Proceedings when Their Parents Divorce or Separate*. London: NSPCC Publications.

Tremlett, G. (2006) 'Spain Attracts Record Levels of Immigrants Seeking Jobs and Sun'. *The Guardian*, 26 July. Available online at: www.guardian.co.uk/world/2006/jul/26/spain.gilestremlett (accessed 5 February 2012).

Turner, G., Harkin, J. and Dawn, T. (2000) *Teaching Young Adults: A Handbook for Teachers in Further Education*. Florence, KY: Routledge.

UK Border Agency (2012) 'Immigration Removal Centres'. Available online at: www.ukba.homeoffice.gov.uk/aboutus/organisation/immigrationremovalcentres/ (accessed 18 February 2012).

UDHR (1948) 'United Nations Universal Declaration of Human Rights'. Available online at: www.un.org/en/documents/udhr/ (accessed 2 February 2012).

UNHCR (2008) 'Global Trends: Refugees, Asylum Seekers, Returnees, Internally Displaced and Stateless Persons'. Available online at: www.unhcr.org/4a375c426.html (accessed 18 February 2012).

UNHCR (2011) *Convention and Protocol Relating to the Status of Refugees*. Geneva: UNHCR Communications and Public Information Service.

Walters, S. (2012) 'Secret Report Warns of Migration Meltdown in Britain'. *Daily Mail*. Available online at: www.dailymail.co.uk/news/article-398232/Secret-report-warns-migration-meltdown-Britain.html#ixzz1lVCWCsXe (accessed 5 February 2012).

Ware, J. (2009) 'Yes Family Breakdown IS behind Broken Britain'. *Daily Mail*, 11 July. Available online at: www.dailymail.co.uk/debate/article-1198962/Yes-family-breakdown-IS-broken-Britain-Top-judge-says-national-tragedy-attacks-BBC-suppressing-debate.html (accessed 30 December 2011).

Weedon, C. (2004) *Identity and Culture: Narratives of Difference and Belonging*. Berkshire: McGraw-Hill Education.

Williams, J., Williams, C. and Johnson, M. R. D. (2010) *Race and Ethnicity in a Welfare Society*. Berkshire: McGraw-Hill Education.

World Bank (2010) *World Development Indicators 2010*. Herndon, VA: World Bank Publications.

Wright, O. (2011) 'Labour Accuses Cameron of Double Standards over "Runaway Dads"'. Available online at: www.independent.co.uk/news/uk/politics/labour-accuses-cameron-of-double-standards-over-runaway-dads-2299927.html (accessed 21 June 2011).

Younger, M., McLellan, R. and Warrington, M. (2005) *Raising Boys' Achievement in Secondary Schools*. Berkshire, UK: McGrawHill Education.

Web-sites

www.adoptionuk.org/information/100172/100262/102993/who_can_adopt/ (accessed 8 January 2012).

www.archives.gov/exhibits/charters/declaration_transcript.html (accessed 2 February 2012).

www.baaf.org.uk/info/adoption (accessed 12 February 2012).

www.bbc.co.uk/health/physical_health/family/stepfamilies/step_becoming.shtml (accessed 8 August 2011).

www.bemyparent.org.uk/features/attachment-issues-in-adoption-and-foster-care,65,AR.html (accessed 7 November 211).

www.education.gov.uk/childrenandyoungpeople/families/childpoverty/a0066298/ child-poverty (accessed 21 May 2011).

www.education.gov.uk/inthenews/inthenews/a0070284/focus-on-families-new-drive-to-help-troubled-families (accessed 22 May 2011).

www.education.gov.uk/rsgateway/DB/SFR/s000968/index.shtml (accessed 28 August 2011).

www.fostering.net/ (accessed 14 February 2012).

www.guardian.co.uk/business/2007/apr/12/businessglossary38 (accessed 18 August 2011).

www.immigrationmatters.co.uk/as-east-european-workers-leave-uk-in-droves-what-effect-will-the-exodus-have-on-the-care-sector.html (accessed 5 February 2012).

www.justiceforfamilies.freeforums.org/adoption-finally-admitting-it-destroys-children-t3436.html (accessed 12 February 2012).

www.legislation.gov.uk/ukpga/1998/42/schedule/1 (accessed 2 February 2012).

www.minimumincomestandard.org (accessed 17 August 2011).

www.mix-d.org/about/our-contribution-to-the-discussion (accessed 16 February 2012).

www.nottinghamshire.gov.uk/home/learningandwork/caringforchildren/adoption/ beingadopted.htm (accessed 8 January 2012).

www.poverty.org.uk/16/index.shtml?2 (accessed 20 May 2011).

www.pre-school.org.uk/practitioners/inclusion/544/how-can-we-support-the-identities-of-our-mixed-heritage-children (accessed 12 February 2012).

www.refugeecouncil.org.uk/practice/basics/process (accessed 4 February 2012).

www.scope.org.uk/about-us/our-brand/talking-about-disability/social-model-disability (accessed 12 February 2012).

www.telegraph.co.uk/education/educationnews/8272027/Ofsted-white-boys-held-back-by-low-expectations.html (accessed 2 February 2012).

www.thesun.co.uk/sol/homepage/news/article4098815.ece (accessed 5 February 2012).

www.ukdp.co.uk/changing-your-childs-name/#adoption#ixzz1J1W9EUZy (accessed 12 February 2012).

www.un.org/en/documents/udhr/ (accessed 2 February 2012).

www.unstats.un.org/unsd/mdg/Metadata.aspx?IndicatorId=0&SeriesId=584 (accessed 18 August 2011).

www.winstonswish.org.uk/mainsection.asp?section=000100010004&pagetitle=About+Us (accessed 10 August 2011).

Index